Foreword by Best-Selling Author
and Co-Founder of the Oneness Movement, Sri Preethaji

THE SOVEREIGN WOMAN'S WAY

A TRANSFORMATIONAL JOURNEY OF SELF LOVE & EMPOWERMENT

JOANNE OMER

The Sovereign Woman's Way
A Transformational Journey of Self Love & Empowerment

joanneomer.com

Copyright © 2025 Joanne Omer

Published by Made to Change the World™ Publishing
Nashville, TN

ISBN: 978-1-956837-46-9 Print
        978-1-956837-47-6 ebook

Printed in the USA, Canada, Australia, and Europe

I dedicate this book to love.

Love is the only thing that is real.

Contents

ACKNOWLEDGMENTS

I would like to acknowledge and express my gratitude to all the teachers I have had who have walked the path before me and helped make that path clearer.

I want to thank Tony Robbins for his incredible vision, tenacity, resilience, leadership, and unstoppable determination to make a difference in the lives of millions of people. I also want to acknowledge his beautiful wife and partner, Sage Robbins, who has been a powerful force in teaching me about all the flavors and expressions of love.

Thank you for showing me what is possible through love and devotion to a cause that is greater than myself.

I extend my thanks to Vianna Stibal for her amazing gift of ThetaHealing® that she has brought to the world. It has made a phenomenal difference in my life, my connection with the Creator, my own healing journey, and in my ability to support and heal others.

My gratitude goes out to Sheila Kelley for her teachings on embracing the love of my beautiful and erotic body!

I appreciate and acknowledge the faculty and leaders of the Oneness Movement, especially Sri Krishnaji and Sri Preethaji, for providing me with the tools to live in a beautiful state and for reminding me that there are only two states: a beautiful state or a suffering state.

To all the women who have laughed with me, danced with me, and held me through my tears: I am so grateful for each and every one of you for the blessing you are in my life. I would not be the woman I am today without you.

To all the souls in the form of the divine masculine that have touched my life, cracked open my heart, loved and supported me, cheered me on, recognized my beauty, and provided words of encouragement. This book would not have been possible without you, your essence, and the impact you have had on me. You allowed me to feel what love is, and for that, I am immensely grateful.

And to the man who has been at my side through all the ups and downs; who has been my biggest teacher, lover, champion, and challenger; and who lovingly tolerates my crazy ideas, concepts, and view of the world: my beloved William Omer. You truly are my divine timing soulmate. Thank you for choosing me in this journey of life and for your commitment to our divine purpose.

FOREWORD

Life is an oscillation between chaos and order. And depending on your state of consciousness, your life progresses in either direction.

Joanne Omer's *The Sovereign Woman's Way* invites women to embrace their authentic selves through a journey of self love, awareness, and a deeper connection with oneself, the divine, and all life. Sri Krishnaji and I teach a foundational insight necessary for anyone to embark on a spiritual journey: Every human being either lives in a suffering state or a no-suffering state. There is no third state. And the most important decision you ever make in life is: In what state do I want to respond to challenges and relate to people?

Suffering, to us, is any state that is mentally conflicting and emotionally unpleasant or disturbing. And no-suffering states are states where you are present, your thinking is internally clear, and you are connected. We have taught millions in the world the art of moving from suffering to no-suffering.

This fundamental shift in consciousness from suffering to no-suffering is an absolute must if you are to dissolve the chaos in your personal life and solve the innumerable problems that trouble the world. To this end, Joanne's book is insightful.

One of the central tenets of transformation, as she reiterates again and again in the book, is to connect to your own truth. For, without truth, your aspiration for transformation is merely verbiage. It lacks substance. That is why the ancients exhort all spiritual seekers to journey from untruth to truth, from darkness to light, from fear of death to immortal bliss. For only then is there peace within you. There is peace in the lives of your loved ones, and there is peace in the world.

The Sovereign Woman's Way will guide you toward a deeper sense of harmony with yourself, with others, and with the presence that underlies all existence. May you live a deeply fulfilling life from a beautiful state of consciousness.

Love & Blessings,
Sri Preethaji
Co-founder, Oneness Movement

INTRODUCTION

Thank you for choosing this book. *The Sovereign Woman's Way* is the culmination of years of healing, digging deep, and soul searching to discover who I really am; to open my heart to even more love and beauty; and, most importantly, to embody the woman that I always knew I was deep down inside. This book can help each and every woman to do the same. There is a special reason why this book has ended up in your hands. Whichever way it has come to you, trust that it is the perfect time for you to be reading it. One of the most precious lessons that I have learned in my experience of life is that there are no coincidences; the Creator does not make mistakes. Life is always working out exactly as it is meant to even if it doesn't feel like it at the time.

It was the start of COVID-19 lockdowns in March 2020, and I was trapped in Melbourne, Victoria, in Australia (one of the most locked down cities in the world at that time). And being the eternal optimist that I am, amidst all the chaos that the world was in, I thought to myself, "Wow, this is my opportunity. This is my chance. This is what I've been preparing for. I am being forced to stay at home and focus on my mission, my purpose to make a difference! This is my time to share my knowledge and my gifts!" Being locked down in my home was an opportunity for me to get my message out there, to help people, to teach them about health and wellness and healing. There had never been a more befitting time. I was in my element, and there were finally no distractions. I went at it, like everything in my life. Full steam ahead!

During 2020, I developed the very first instructor training program for KunYin®, a feminine movement practice that I had created in 2019. Kun in KunYin® stands for the kundalini energy that flows through everyone, and Yin is for the feminine aspect of the yin yang. KunYin® is a feminine movement modality designed to support women to embrace and embody all aspects of themselves, to move energy and emotion through the body, and to get women out of their heads and connect them into the power and wisdom of their body. The powerful combination of free movement, energy healing, and psychosomatics has created incredible change and transformation in women's confidence, esteem, and connection with themselves. I started teaching online, and it soon became a very busy time since I already had a successful business selling essential oils and wellness products as well as a coaching business. I reveled in the focus and energy I could give my clients, students, and team members. During this period, I helped people start their own businesses with the oils and through coaching. As lockdowns had also created significant strain on relationships, many people were reaching out to me for relationship coaching. I was so inspired to be doing all the things I loved; my business had tripled. I was working over fourteen hours a day—from the moment I woke up until my head hit the pillow at night for more than seven months. I felt like I was unstoppable. I finally had all the time in the world to focus, to buckle down, and to do all the things that I had always wanted to do.

Operating at that pace felt good (for a while), but it wasn't sustainable. Fast-forward to October 2021 when I contracted COVID-19, and everything came to a grinding halt. I had not been sick for years and years; in fact, I had prided myself on being someone who never gets sick! So contracting the virus and being bedridden for three weeks was a massive shock to my system as well as my ego. Working in the heath, healing, and wellness space, I had a deeply flawed and limiting belief that

I wasn't supposed to get sick, that I was infallible. So when I did, it hit me hard on many levels.

I lost my sense of smell, and as a distributor for an essential oils company, that was problematic. How could I share or promote a product that I couldn't smell?

I felt defeated. I still had my beautiful KunYin® to focus on and grow. But the oils had been such a big part of my life and my entrepreneurial identity that without them, I felt lost. So when the state of Victoria, as well as the rest of the world, started to ease up on lockdown restrictions, one of my dear friends suggested I come to the United Kingdom and spend some time with her. Another friend decided to join me on my upcoming adventure, so, without hesitation, I booked my flight to London knowing that what I needed more than anything was connection to aid in my recovery and rejuvenation.

Once we landed, we were immediately whisked away to a spa in the heart of Longleat Forest, where we had massages; connected with the giant redwoods, other trees, plants, and animals; and satisfied a deep need for freedom, adventure, and awe. It was beautiful. I remember feeling my entire body exhale and thinking, "Finally . . . I can relax." I felt more like myself than I had in months.

Our next stop was to visit a friend of a friend on the Isle of Wight who had lovingly arranged for a massage therapist to come and meet us where we were staying. During that massage, something strange happened to me that had never happened before. I felt a rush of energy enter through the palms of my hands and travel all the way through my body as if bolts of electricity were flowing through me.

My whole body was tingling and alive with energy.

WTF was that? When my friend suggested we book in again for the following day I said, "Hell yes, book me in!"

For the days and weeks that followed, my body began to slowly awaken. I felt a sense of aliveness that I had never experienced before. I felt joy, love, and bliss; my whole body was alive with these sensations! I had known joy and love before, but never had they felt like this.

It was euphoric; I felt high. I felt high on life. I felt connected to the highest forms of love and joy—the energy of unconditional love, the love that can only come from the source of creation. Some people describe this as a kundalini awakening. Whatever it was, I loved how it felt, and I knew that I wanted to experience more of it!

More than two weeks had passed since my arrival in the United Kingdom, and even though I was only getting two or three hours of sleep a night, I wasn't tired. I had an abundance of energy! Our adventures led us to the lands of Cornwall, a magical place with tales of knights, giants, fairies, pixies, and mermaids. I remember one night lying in my bed wide awake at 4:00 am, my whole body tingling, sweating, and feeling alive in all places, if you know what I mean! My whole body was orgasmic!

One day, we spent some time walking through a beautiful fern gully with a little creek and a waterfall. It was so heartening to be in nature and to experience life in the present moment without any time constraints, without needing to be anywhere in particular. When we departed this piece of paradise on Earth, we walked through a field toward a narrow road. As I walked alongside the road on a stony path, I was filled with joy and gratitude. Out of the corner of my eye, something got my attention. I stopped to look, and as I turned my head, I saw a long, gangly stick creature that looked like the stones. Once noticed, it scurried away and disappeared into the rocks. I could not believe my eyes! I burst into tears, not from fear or sadness, but from sheer joy. I believe that in that moment I saw a beautiful creature from beyond the veil, an elemental. I

4

remembered the words of my teacher Vianna Stibal that fairy creatures only show themselves to those that are pure of heart, and I let the tears of gratitude fall. Now, some of you reading this may think that I have lost my mind. If I was reading this ten years ago, I would have thought the same! But I know what I saw was very real. Something inside of me was changing. I was changed.

On our last day in Cornwall before the drive home, we stopped by the village of Tintagel and sat on top of a beautiful grassy knoll overlooking Merlin's Cave. I could smell the ocean breeze carrying the beautiful fresh scent of the lawn beneath me. I . . . could . . . smell . . . the ocean breeze. I could smell again; my sense of smell that I had taken for granted had been returned to me.

I felt such a deep sense of gratitude and appreciation at that moment. I felt a deep sense of love in my heart that I had never felt before. I felt my connection with the Creator, with God. I felt a connection with myself, my beauty, my divinity, and I wanted to hold on to that feeling for as long as I could. I would do anything to have it!

When I finally returned home to Australia, I was alive again. However, I wasn't the same person who had left. No longer did the hustle and bustle of city living excite or inspire me. I felt constrained by the city, my home, my commitments, my responsibilities and obligations. I needed to be free again, like I had been in the United Kingdom. And I wanted to understand what that feeling was and how to cultivate it for myself, how to bring it to me rather than go out looking for it. So I committed to giving myself the space and time to find out what it was. The following year, 2023, I would go away again . . . to find answers!

For the months that followed, I went to some of the darkest places that I'd ever been. What goes up must come down, and boy did I feel the downs. I have never cried so much in my entire life. I didn't know what was happening to me. At one point, I thought that maybe I was losing my grip on reality and would never feel normal again.

But still I was obsessed with the feeling I had felt during my time in the United Kingdom. I wanted to pursue that sense of love, connection, and aliveness that I knew was available to me, that I knew I could access again. But to do that, I realized I had to be willing to let go of my life as I knew it.

My desire for love, connection, and freedom led me to that point, and I needed to love myself enough to continue on that journey. To go on it, I had to put myself first. I had to have a deep sense of who I was and know that I was worthy and deserving of that kind of love. I had to be willing to risk everything for it: my relationship with my husband and twenty-one years of marriage; the opinion of my family and their judgment; the guilt of not spending time with them doing what a "good" daughter, wife, sister, and aunty "should" do; the potential impact on my relationship coaching business and clients, as I worried what they would think of me if I didn't have the "perfect" relationship.

I had known for a long time that my purpose in life was to lead the way for humanity to awaken to higher levels of consciousness. I also fundamentally believed that my life was for serving others, and that was, in part, why my husband and I were not able to naturally have children of our own. I knew that I was born to serve humanity in a different way and make a difference in the world around me and beyond. I knew that through my healing and my transformation that I would share what I learned with my students, my clients, and anyone who would listen!

I was bare, exposed, and vulnerable. There was no one who I felt I could talk to. My husband had just lost his mother only months prior, and my "awakening" was also taking a huge toll on his health and wellbeing. But I knew that whatever I was doing was for a higher purpose. It wasn't just for me, but first it needed to be for me. Everything else had to be stripped away.

Every conversation, healing, and action I took led me to experience a deeper sense of love for myself. For me to take those actions, I had to be willing to put myself first at every single moment because that was what I wanted. I knew that whatever I was experiencing and learning I would, in turn, use in service of others.

I know now that my life is lived in devotion to love and to humanity. I want each person to experience and live life how they want to, on their terms. To do all that with grace, compassion, kindness and without guilt or shame takes a profound sense of courage! I had to face some of my deepest fears, heal some of my deepest wounds, and learn valuable lessons.

If you have chosen this book, you may be feeling called to a deeper experience of love. You might feel like something is missing from your life though you can't quite put your finger on it. Love may seem elusive, like you will never find "the one" or anyone who comes close. You may have given up on love if your heart has been shattered into a million pieces and you doubt it can ever be whole again. Maybe you have been hurt, betrayed, or abandoned in love and are afraid to love again. You may know that you are loved but struggle to feel or receive it. Maybe you have given away your life to be in service of others to the detriment of your own happiness. Maybe you have resigned yourself to the fact that this is just the way life is.

Wherever you are on this journey, know that as of right now, you are exactly where you are meant to be. You are here so that you can elevate your experience of love and life. Understand that all things are possible, and you have the strength to overcome any obstacles that stand in your way to living in your authentic truth and power, however that looks for you! Everyone has their own unique purpose to bring to this world. *The*

Sovereign Woman's Way will support you to find yours and guide you through this time.

This book may challenge you, and you may resist what it says or feel the need to take a break. Do what you need to do and reflect on what is happening for you when that resistance rises. Don't run away from it; it is part of the work that needs to be done. Lean into it. What are you feeling? Name it. When you are on the precipice of transformation in your life, fear will arise. This is completely normal, so don't let that stop you from moving forward with your dreams. Everything you desire is on the other side of your fear.

Love is a powerful force that will lead you through darkness to your inner light.

This is an initiation into self love and the continued opening of your heart. If you're willing to dive deep into it, do the work, and explore the places that you don't want to go, then you too can experience the feeling I am talking about. If you are willing to walk the path of your soul regardless of your fears and let go of anything that you think you already know, then this journey is for you. You will experience yourself as someone who has faith and courage. You will experience yourself as someone who is devoted to love and who is the walking, talking embodiment of authentically living in your truth.

Trust that the timing of *The Sovereign Woman's Way* is perfect. Trust that now is the time for you to receive the messages, wisdom, lessons, and insights within these pages. The journey itself is the destination. The only place you ever really arrive is your grave—and you wanna make sure that by that time, you can say you lived your best freakin' life, a life that you consciously created and that you are proud of!

In being present, healing, and embracing change, your life can become a magical masterpiece beyond your wildest dreams, and you don't have to leave your country, your home, or your family to find it. All the answers lay within you. This book will help you reveal the parts of you that are holding you back from all that you desire. What the Creator has in store for you, and what your soul has prepared for you, is truly incredible. Now it's your turn to do the work, elevate your consciousness, and align with the highest possibilities for yourself in this lifetime. Everything your heart desires is within reach.

## CHAPTER 1

The Foundational Principles

The teachings, wisdom, lessons, and insights in this book will help you discover the power to create the life you always desired. In doing so, you'll experience the deepest love for yourself, which, in turn, will attract even more love and joy to you!

But first, there are some foundational principles that you need to understand and embody. These are the keys to discovering your innate sovereign power and experiencing more love, connection, and fulfillment in life. Many people seek more and more knowledge, but, often, knowledge alone makes no difference in the experience and quality of your life. Some say that knowledge is power, but I believe that knowledge is not power unless you act upon it. Embodying the knowledge you acquire means not only comprehending it in your mind but also bringing it into your reality through who you are being.

Gaining knowledge is the easy part; the practical embodiment of that knowledge is the most challenging yet most impactful undertaking in creating positive change in your life.

If you are willing to do the inner work, you will heal the wounds that have held you back from experiencing the love you deserve. You will unlock the doors to the wisdom of self mastery and create more love for yourself and those around you.

Through the work, you'll uncover the underlying reasons for past struggles in life and love and learn how to release them to attract more passion, creativity, connection, and joy into your life.

You will understand how you became who you are today and examine the beliefs that have either empowered or disempowered you in love and life. You'll knock down the barriers to finding balance in life and break free from cycles that hold you captive. *The Sovereign Woman's Way* will introduce you to the universal laws that, once you are conscious of them, will support your growth and bring you into the natural flow of life.

First, you must believe in something greater than yourself. Yes, you are powerful beyond your wildest imagination, and there is a force that created you that is more knowing and powerful than you. Throughout the pages of this book, I may refer to this force as God, the Creator, the Universe, Source, the Divine, or Unconditional Love. Here, this being is one and the same. You don't have to believe in any particular religion to get the most out of this book, but you do need to believe in something greater than yourself. In order to access this divine source of love, you must believe that there is *something* or *someone* who loves you so much they created you. A source of love that is unlimited, that doesn't rely on external circumstances or your behavior to be received. You didn't have to do anything to deserve this love; it was a gift given through the creation of your life. There is a governing energy that created all living beings. And this leads to the next principle—energy!

Everything Is Energy!

Energy is the fundamental essence that permeates everything in the Universe. In its highest form, it is the invisible force that harmoniously binds all matter and life together. When you consider yourself and the world around you, you see a complex interplay of energy in the form of matter. Your body, the objects you interact with, even the air you breathe are all composed of matter, which, in turn, is made up of atoms and molecules. These atoms and molecules are constantly moving, creating your unique vibration and blueprint in the world. Even the thoughts and feelings you have carry a certain type of energy and vibration.

Bear with me because this is about as scientific as I'm gonna get. As you delve deeper into the composition of matter, you find subatomic particles such as protons, neutrons, and electrons, all buzzing with energy. These particles are held together by powerful forces within the atom, creating a dynamic dance of energy fields. Even the seemingly empty space between particles is filled with energy, creating an interconnected web of energy that defines your physical reality here on Earth.

Understanding that everything is ultimately energy in various forms is a foundational principle that underlies the teachings in this book. By recognizing the energetic nature of the Universe and yourself, you can begin to explore the profound implications of energy and vibration in shaping your experiences and interactions with the world.

Essentially, energy is the essence of your existence, the invisible thread that connects you to the fabric of the Universe, to other people, and to your Creator. You are never really separate; you are always connected to everything and everyone through this pulsing web of energy. When you are balanced and in harmony, you can experience the magic of this connection.

The Magical Trinity of Body, Mind, and Soul

Now that you understand the incredible energy force that created you, let's look at the three-dimensional intersection of how your body, mind, and soul work together, or as I like to say, the Magical Trinity of Body, Mind, and Soul. I like the magical trinity metaphor because when you align these three aspects of yourself and allow them to work together in harmony, life moves from the natural to the supernatural. If you want to create any lasting and meaningful change, a holistic approach to your evolution is essential. Many healing modalities focus just on the spirit and doing soul work. Soul work is absolutely necessary, but it alone will not create lasting change. Working with just the spirit can create disconnection from your Earthly body, and you become head-in-the-clouds (so to speak) and not grounded in reality. You cannot impact reality if you are not connected to it and living in it. Likewise, connection to the body alone cannot create a sovereign life. Physical movement practices such as gym work, exercise regimens, dancing, boxing, and Pilates can create incredible feelings of wellbeing and aliveness; however, if you solely focus on them, you'll neglect the mind and the soul. Moreover, while there are many programs, books, courses, and seminars that you can take to master the mind, focusing on the mind alone can leave you feeling unfulfilled, lacking passion, pleasure, vitality, and connection. Doing only mental work can also cause you to burn out. This is why there needs to be a connection between the mind, body, and soul in order for you to feel all the joy that is possible as a soul in a physical body. You are a multidimensional being, and all your dimensions must be integrated so that you experience love in its fullness. You will grow to understand more about this mind, body, and soul connection in the coming chapter's section on the thinking-feeling feedback loop!

To live life here on this planet as a human being, you need a physical body. In my experience in the somatic movement space (KunYin®) and as a psychosomatic therapist, I have learned that many in society, especially women, are disconnected from their bodies. What I mean is that many people have dissociated from their emotional and feeling body. They think their way through life, not allowing a balance of thinking *and* feeling to guide them. The body is always speaking to you, and to hear its whispers, you need to slow down and allow its wisdom to be heard. Sometimes the body needs to scream in physical pain before people are willing to stop and give it their awareness and attention. When you predominantly use the logical, thinking, analytical part of yourself, you disconnect from the intuitive, feeling, and emotional part—the body. The analytical part of you is your masculine energy and the feeling part of you is your feminine energy. Further into this chapter, you will find a detailed breakdown on the differences between masculine and feminine principles.

The body is the history book of everything that you have ever experienced throughout your life. From the moment of conception to growing in your mother's womb, you were feeling and absorbing the world around you. If your mother's pregnancy with you was joyful, peaceful, and happy, then you would have felt those feelings. Conversely, if your mother's pregnancy was stressful, abusive, fearful, or violent, then you would have felt that too. Every experience you have had in this physical body has shaped you physically, mentally, emotionally, and spiritually. The shape of your bones to the texture of the tissue under your skin to your physical appearance, the way you walk, your stance and gestures have all been shaped by your life experiences. Deep within your cellular memory, the emotions and feelings of the experiences that you have had exist. Your body is so much more than a meat suit; it is a walking, talking encyclopedia filled with wisdom that most people rarely connect with or know on a deep level.

By understanding the wisdom of your body and recognizing how he or she is feeling (yes, I believe your body has its own unique identity!), you can delve into a deeper understanding of yourself. Through acknowledging and accepting the lower vibrational emotions, like grief, shame, and anger to name a few, you will be on your way to transcending them. I am not shaming the lower vibrational emotions. All emotions are beautiful and welcome; each produces a different vibration and, therefore, different behaviors and outcomes in life. Connecting with all the emotions you experience allows you to truly know yourself and move through any emotional barriers that hold you back from living a harmonious, joyful, and fulfilling life.

To learn how to shift from overthinking to embracing your body's wisdom, you can access my free meditation at thesovereignwomansway.com. This meditation is designed to get you out of your thoughts and into the wisdom of your body and heart.

This may feel a little controversial, but the current generation and thousands of past generations have been raised in a patriarchal world where the masculine has been the head of communities, organizations, and families. This has led to a suppression of feminine aspects, including emotions and, consequently, feelings. Considering that you need your body to receive and process what you feel, when you disconnect from it, you are essentially disconnecting from over fifty percent of *yourself*. Instead, for centuries, more importance has been placed on the logical, analytical, and thinking mind rather than the emotional, feeling body, thus allowing the mind and its thoughts to run your life. I don't know about you, but some of the thoughts that go through my mind at times are better left unthought and unsaid! This is especially relevant if you have an overactive mind that tends to spiral or if you suffer from anxiety or depression.

To live life powerfully as a sovereign woman, you need to have a healthy relationship with both your masculine and feminine energies. These need to be aligned, working together, and integrated. This is the holy grail of transformation. When you can operate from a place of balance and integration of these energies, you can experience choices that empower you, including harmony within yourself that will flow into every aspect of your life.

If this resonates with you, listen up because you will want to know how your mind actually works. As you move through this book and heal, you may very well find that you resolve some of the emotions and feelings that are keeping you trapped in old patterns and start to feel lighter and lighter!

Let's go a little deeper into the mind without getting too brainy and scientific! At a basic level, the mind has a conscious and subconscious, where *sub* means below consciousness. I like to say that what resides in the subconscious is what you don't know and you don't know that you don't know it! And your consciousness is what you know that you know and you know that you know it!

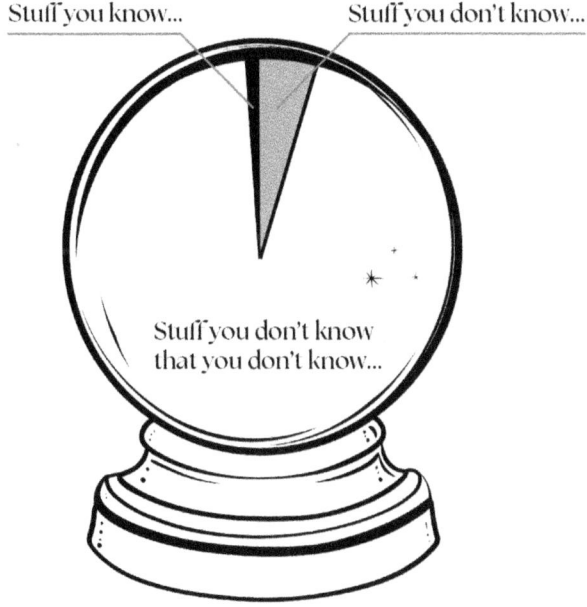

Stuff you know...

Stuff you don't know...

Stuff you don't know that you don't know...

From the time that you were conceived until today, your brain has been receiving downloads of information about the world around you and who you are in relation to it. These downloads of information create fundamental behaviors, beliefs, values, and attitudes that have become "hardwired" as synaptic pathways in your subconscious mind. These pathways are dynamic and ongoing throughout your life. You replay the patterns associated with these pathways automatically daily, rarely stopping to think about how you actually became this way.

Have you ever blurted out something without thinking and thought to yourself, "Oh my goodness, I sound just like my mother/father?" This is a good example of how these subconscious downloads have shaped you and are governing your thoughts, feelings, and behaviors. Although not scientifically proven, some sources suggest that the subconscious makes up a significant portion of your overall mental capacity, possibly ranging from ninety to ninety-five percent!

You might not even be aware of what is driving you to think, feel, and act in a certain way! Remember, you don't know that you don't know. When I discovered this, it really blew my mind and made me very curious to find out what was lying there, hidden, beneath my consciousness!

Essentially, until your subconscious comes into your consciousness, you are on autopilot, living out the thousands of hardwired pathways of programming. I call this your conditioning. This is why you may wonder why life sometimes feels like Groundhog Day; why you keep meeting the same people, facing the same challenges, and getting the same results. Nothing changes if nothing changes! More often than not, you did not choose these patterns, beliefs, and behaviors—you were conditioned to be this way. Until you become aware of them, they will control you. Once you become aware and they rise into the consciousness, then you can actively choose to change them.

Your beliefs have the capacity to empower you or disempower you. There are empowering beliefs that you may want to identify and retain. There also are disempowering beliefs, referred to as limiting beliefs, that may have served you at one time in your life but now seem to be limiting you in life, love, and the results you currently can attain.

If your beliefs govern many of your thoughts, feelings, and behaviors, and you don't know that you don't know them, they are pretty powerful in running your day-to-day life. Let's examine a little bit more about belief systems—what they are and how you create them.

Belief Systems

According to one of my very precious and wise teachers, Vianna Stibal, the founder of ThetaHealing®, you have four different types of belief systems: core, genetic, historical, and soul.

CORE

The core belief system is formed by beliefs that you create from the time you are in your mother's womb until the present day. These beliefs are about yourself and the world around you. They are largely shaped by your life experiences, cultural background, upbringing, environment, schooling, and friendships. These factors influence the core beliefs you hold. According to Dr. Rima Laibow and noted by Dr. Bruce Lipton in his book *The Biology of Belief*, children from ages two to seven use theta brain waves, those between four to eight hertz. This is also the brain wave frequency used by hypnotherapists to create a more suggestive state. So you could conclude that children between the ages of two and seven are like little sponges, taking in the world around them and developing those subconscious, hardwired neural pathways mentioned earlier. As you grow older, you become less susceptible to outside influences, and by the time you have reached adolescence, you have a full set of downloaded programs that create who you are based on who you believe yourself to be.

I recall a moment in my childhood when I was confident I knew the answer to a question at school. I eagerly raised my hand and blurted out the answer before the teacher even called upon me, only to get it wrong. I was so embarrassed. At that moment, I felt small, and I remember scolding myself with the words, "I'm such an idiot, I am so stupid." This moment created a core belief that has stayed with me for a very long time in my subconscious. In fact, any time I felt embarrassed since or got something "wrong," I would repeat those words to myself. On the other hand, my mother was very supportive and taught me that I could achieve anything I set my mind to. So I grew up with another core belief that I could do anything! In essence, I had unknowingly, over the course of my childhood, created conflicting beliefs—one suggesting inadequacy and the other promoting limitless potential.

To uncover core beliefs, reflect on some of the most prominent memories from your childhood. They may be happy or unhappy memories. In my experience working with thousands of clients, I have found in many cases that when they still have a strong recollection and emotional connection with these experiences, there is an imprint of subconscious beliefs that have shaped who they are today.

Genetic

The genetic level of belief systems delves into the inheritance of traits and tendencies from your parents through your DNA. Regardless of whether you like it or not, you are your parents! Your body serves as a repository of not just your own experiences, but also the cellular memories that are carried through from your ancestors. These inherited beliefs, passed down through generations, can shape your subconscious mind and influence your outlook on life.

For example, my family history includes my grandfather's upbringing on the remote island of Alicudi, where survival demanded hard work and resilience due to its harsh conditions. Reflecting this legacy, I worked tirelessly from a young age, holding multiple jobs and managing several businesses. While initially believing hard work was necessary for success, I later chose to release that belief. Instead, I embraced a more balanced approach to life and replaced the old belief with, "I can work with ease and joy and still be successful."

By acknowledging and understanding these inherited beliefs, you can consciously decide which ones to hold on to and which ones to let go of. Through self reflection, you can examine whether you inherited your beliefs from your ancestors and your genetics.

Dedicate some time to journaling about the following areas of your life: money and finances, religion and culture, sex and intimacy, morals and values.

As you reflect, ask yourself:

♡ What do I believe about each of these areas based upon what I've seen through my family? For example:

- Money is hard to come by.
- It is wrong to have sex before marriage.
- Marriage is forever.
- You must be kind even if people are unkind to you.
- It is shameful to enjoy sex.
- I must put other people's needs before mine.
- It's hard work to make money.
- Rich people are greedy.

♡ How have these beliefs impacted your life?

If you wish to delve deeper and discover what beliefs are lurking in your subconscious mind, you can use a muscle testing technique to test if you hold them; detailed instructions are available at thesovereignwomansway. com. Additionally, lists of common limiting beliefs that you may not even know and don't know that you hold are available there and in Chapter 11.

Another way to discover what inherited beliefs you may have subconsciously taken on is to have conversations with your family members. Some questions you could ask them are:

♥ What was life like for you growing up?

♥ What was your parents' relationship like?

♥ What did your parents believe about money?

  • Did they have a little?/Did they have a lot?

This process of self discovery empowers you to break free from limiting beliefs and align with your true self for personal growth and fulfillment.

HISTORICAL

The next level of beliefs pertains to those held at the historical level. According to Vianna Stibal's book *ThetaHealing*®, the historical level is divided into two parts: past lives and group consciousness. In past lives, beliefs are carried at a soul level through various lifetimes and different incarnations.

Having been raised in a Catholic family, I was never encouraged to believe in past lives. It was frowned upon, and discussing it was discouraged and shut down, leading to a sense of shame for any beliefs I held that differed from this view. However, through my healing journey and life experiences, I have gradually let go of those limiting beliefs that no longer serve me. I encourage you to think objectively about some of the beliefs that you have inherited and have an open mind. Becoming a sovereign woman is to find your own wisdom; what reigns true for you? What feels right in your heart and soul? I have come to realize that some of my beliefs were not even my own and often made no logical sense. Certain fears and reactions seemed to have no explanation unless they were rooted in past experiences.

Through past life regressions, I have felt a strong connection to previous incarnations on Earth and elsewhere. For instance, I was afraid of Native American cries. When I heard them, they would terrify me. I had no idea why; it was strange that they would have such an effect on me. But at a healing session in 2023, I uncovered a past life where I was a young Native American woman accidentally shot with an arrow into my back by my own people during a civil war. I suddenly understood my fear. When I went a little deeper into this lifetime, I was in love with a white man, and he witnessed me dying. What I learned from this lifetime was forgiveness, and I was reminded of how deeply and passionately I have loved. I even noticed that I have a little birthmark on my back in exactly the same spot where the deadly arrow entered my body.

Going back into past lives can be fun, but it can also lead you down a rabbit hole that doesn't really serve any purpose. Therefore, when you resolve past lives, it is important to look back and reflect and discover the lessons of the lifetime. What did you learn? How could this learning benefit you in your life today?

By resolving my past life traumas, I have been able to release the associated pain and fears, carrying forward only the lessons learned. Journaling and other self reflection processes will help you to access some of the beliefs and lessons learned from your past lives. Alternatively, if you prefer to have someone guide you, see a trained ThetaHealing® practitioner to support you through this process. For a list of recommended healers, visit thesovereignwomansway.com.

Beliefs at the historical level also encompass group consciousness, which consists of beliefs collectively held by groups of people that individuals may adopt. It is like being surrounded by many Wi-Fi routers, with people as the receivers connecting to the beliefs of the group consciousness. Examples of group consciousness include churches, religions, political parties, and other organizations that uphold specific beliefs and ideologies.

SOUL

Your soul is beautiful, infinite, and radiating energy originating from a realm beyond your Earthly existence. In this lifetime, you bring fragments of your soul with you. Due to the ethereal nature of your soul's energy, it cannot fully inhabit your physical body, as your body is too dense to contain its entirety. Instead, you carry a portion of this soul energy with you as you go through your life.

At times, beliefs can be ingrained at the level of the soul, representing the essence of who you are. When you undergo profound emotional experiences, face tragic losses, or encounter deeply impactful events, these beliefs can become embedded at the core of your being. For instance, beliefs like "love is painful" or "love hurts" may take root at the soul level.

I recall an impactful personal experience. When I was nineteen, I fell in love for the first time, only to have my partner betray me. The profound heartache and pain I felt led me to adopt the belief that love inevitably brings pain and heartbreak. The rejection and abandonment had such a profound impact on me that this belief became deeply rooted within my soul.

Typically, when you have emotional releases and shed tears, you are undergoing healing at the soul level. In such moments, sending yourself unconditional, healing love from your heart can be a powerful gesture of support and compassion. For more, experience the free Unconditional Love Healing Meditation for Healing of the Soul at thesovereignwomansway.com.

CONFLICTING AND OUTDATED BELIEFS

Reflecting on these concepts, consider the four levels of belief systems—core, genetic, historical, and soul—and how they manifest in your own life. Realize that some of your beliefs might conflict, which can create a lot of confusion and discord. The subconscious mind and the neural pathways that you have created can be likened to a ball of yarn—many beliefs that are all tangled up together. Recall my earlier story: I had subconsciously created the belief that I am an idiot, but I also had a belief that I can do anything.

Such internal conflict between negative and positive beliefs can hinder your progress in life, leading to a cycle of starting and stopping, especially when you are venturing into new territories and uncertainty. This conflict can often manifest in the body as psychosomatic ailments and impact the body's structure, tissue quality, mobility, and how you move through life mentally, emotionally, and physically. But, by learning about and identifying belief systems, you can begin to untangle them and gain more clarity on who you are and how you became that person. Untangled and clear, you will be able to move forward in life with more confidence and certainty.

Also, be aware that you likely hold some beliefs that you once considered noble and, indeed, probably served you up to a point in your life. Perhaps they got you through a difficult time or enabled you to survive or be loved and accepted. "What doesn't kill you makes you stronger" is an example of a belief that, while serving you, can also create painful patterns of struggle in order to become stronger. A much higher-serving belief would be, "I can become stronger without struggle or pain!" I encourage you to question all your beliefs. Do they still serve you in the life you want to create today?

Ponder the beliefs you have internalized that stem from teachings, experiences, or self perceptions. Beliefs like "I am stupid" can impede your capacity to love, while convictions like "I must work hard" may obstruct your ability to prioritize self care and wellbeing. Recognize that any belief that restricts or limits you has the potential to disrupt your journey toward profound self love and acceptance. Understanding this, work to embrace the idea that you are inherently perfect, whole, and complete, just as you are.

In my three-month signature program, also called "The Sovereign Woman's Way," I spend time diving deeper into the limiting beliefs that you hold at each of the levels and help you to clear them so that you can create even more love and acceptance in your life.

To further explore these concepts, you can access a complimentary Belief Systems workbook on my website at thesovereignwomansway.com.

Emotionality

Feelings stem from emotional states, which are shaped by your thoughts and beliefs. What you think and what you believe generates emotions. You will learn about the interplay between thoughts, beliefs, feelings, and emotions in the following chapter where you'll discover the thinking-feeling feedback loop.

When there is suppression at the emotional level, the ability to feel is restricted. Many individuals find themselves disconnected from their feelings because they have learned to dissociate from their emotions. Dissociation can occur as a response to traumatic experiences, stressful experiences, and from conditioning as a child. This disconnection often arises from a lack of understanding on how to effectively manage emotions, a skill that many have not been taught, not even by their parents. You weren't taught it because your parents were not taught it!

Reflecting on my own experiences as a young girl, I recall many occasions when I would cry, whether due to getting hurt or having a disagreement with my sister. In response, my mother would sternly tell me to stop crying, warning me that she would give me something to cry about. This led me to quickly swallow my tears and subconsciously create the belief that showing emotions, particularly crying, was unacceptable, wrong, and shameful and would mean that I would be punished. This was a moment of disconnection for me. I learned to suppress my emotions and began to see my tears as a sign of weakness.

The pattern of suppressing emotions has been reinforced by societal norms. For example, in a corporate setting, emotional expression is typically not encouraged nor accepted. Imagine being in an office environment and openly releasing anger, frustration, or sadness and receiving praise for doing so. This scenario seems far-fetched because, in reality, such displays of emotion are often viewed as a sign of instability and unreliability and would most certainly hold one back from progressing at work.

I remember believing at one point in my life that it was weak to express sadness. When I was growing up, I saw my mum suffering from anxiety and depression. I didn't want to be like that. I thought I would much rather be like my dad, strong and independent. So I put on a brave face, acted tough, and did not take shit from anyone. It served me for a long time. However, over the years, I became disconnected from myself, from the truth of what I was feeling, and I also found it difficult to authentically have compassion for anyone who was dealing with any pain. It wasn't until I recognized this belief, one of those hardwired neural pathways in my mind that was running in the background, that I could change it and move toward acceptance and compassion.

From a young age, you are taught to suppress the shadow emotions of sadness and anger. The message conveyed is that expressing anger is unacceptable and even dangerous. As a result, you learn to bury your feelings and emotions, eventually numbing yourself to the point where you may no longer feel anything at all. I have worked with many clients and students who were told during their lives that they were too sensitive or too emotional. It has impacted the way they saw themselves, their self confidence and self worth, as well as how they expressed (or didn't express) their emotions. Rarely have human beings been taught to celebrate their emotions, to feel them, experience them, and know that it is okay to have this very human response to life.

Society has created a culture of women and men who ultimately believe that they need to hide their emotions and hide who they really are. You hide away in shame and experience your emotions in secret, or you end up reaching a threshold where your emotions can no longer be contained, more often than not in a river of tears or singeing flames of fire.

As everything is energy and it merely changes form, your emotions need to have somewhere to go when they are experienced. If they are not released, they get stored in your body—in your cells, organs, muscle, and tissues. Over time, this can create physical symptoms such as dis-ease, pain, or inflammation. Your body has an incredible way of communicating with you, and this communication increases and gets louder and louder, particularly when you are not listening or paying attention to what is being said.

This is why I was called to create the KunYin® modality—to support women to get out of their heads and move through the various emotions in their bodies during a sixty-minute movement class. The aim is to create a safe space to move emotions and, therefore, experience more ease, grace, and a flow of energy throughout the body. After all, emotion is simply energy in motion!

Boundaries

Love knows no rules.
Love knows no boundaries.
Love is a law unto itself.
—Joanne Omer

What is a boundary? A boundary is a spoken or unspoken barrier or limit that defines an acceptable behavior or interaction. As each person is different and comes from different backgrounds, cultures, and experiences, setting clear and healthy boundaries is essential in your relationships, both professional and personal. Setting boundaries creates clarity and safety not only for yourself but also for the people around you as they establish the parameters within which you operate in relation to the world around you and with yourself.

Many boundaries are spoken and understood, while others are unspoken and, therefore, easily misunderstood. This lies in the fact that each person has their own unique belief system, genetics, upbringing, and conditioning, all of which influence how they set boundaries and what they consider to be acceptable behavior.

There can also be an emotional toll in setting boundaries with people whose behaviors are not good for you. And standing strong in your decision to set a boundary can be challenging. Sometimes you may wish you didn't need to set a boundary, but deep in your heart you know it is the right, honorable, dignified, brave, and courageous thing to do. Setting boundaries can create deep emotional conflict, grief, guilt, or confusion that needs to be healed and moved through with self compassion and patience.

Learning how to and being okay with saying no is a vital part of boundary setting. Many feelings will arise when you have to say no to someone's request. I know that from my own family conditioning, I was often shamed, told that I was rude, or made to feel guilty when I declined a request or refused to do something that I didn't want to do. My family was not interested in finding out the reasons why I didn't want to do something or having a conversation about it. My mother, in particular, was repeating the family's prevalent genetic conditioning and only doing what she was taught. Little girls were just expected to be good, do as they were told, and not speak unless spoken to! Is it any wonder that so many of Generation X have challenges with healthy self expression?

Before delving into setting boundaries, it is crucial to have a clear understanding of what healthy boundaries entail. Most people have not been taught to identify and set healthy boundaries. It's important to be aware of how cultural norms and family practices shape how you perceive and establish boundaries. Awareness and communication are essential elements of healthy boundary setting.

How do you feel around certain people? Do they make you feel good or do you constantly feel that you are pleasing them and neglecting your own feelings or what is good for you?

Not sure? Check in with your body. How does it feel when you are around certain people? Does it feel calm, peaceful, and at ease? Or does it feel tension, stress, and discomfort?

Communicating how you feel is key when setting boundaries and supports the person to understand how their behavior and actions cause you to feel. It's also important to take responsibility for how you feel and not blame the other person. I always say that no one can make you feel a certain way unless there is something inside of you that it connects with or you allow.

For example, if I came up to you and said, "You have purple eyes," unless you really had purple eyes, you would probably just laugh because you know it's not true. But if I came up to you and said, "You are a selfish bitch," it might sting a little because there may be something within you that wonders if what I say is true and, therefore, triggers a certain feeling or emotion.

A good conversation structure to clarify how you feel and to take responsibility for how you feel while not blaming the other person for your feelings follows:

When you do this (state the behavior),
it makes me feel (describe the body sensations, emotions, and feelings that the behavior triggers inside of you).
I would like (make a request).
If this behavior continues, I will (state your boundary).

For example:

When you raise your voice and yell at me, it makes me feel scared. I experience tightness in my chest. This makes me feel sad, and I want to shut down. I would like to be able to communicate without yelling and complete conversations calmly. If this continues, I will remove myself from the situation until we can communicate calmly.

It is essential to exercise discernment when setting boundaries, considering when and how to establish them with different people. Communicating a boundary should be clear; there should be no doubt that the other person is aware that your boundary has been crossed and what you will and will not tolerate. If a boundary has been crossed repeatedly, then communication to say that you will cease communication may be necessary. Setting a boundary is not the same as cutting someone out of your life without explanation or communication. That is ghosting—a common behavior these days, whereby people cut others from their life without explanation or communication. Listen up, because this is a critical distinction! Ghosting can be really harmful to the wellbeing of both parties. The person who has been ghosted is often left confused and incomplete, wondering what they have done wrong and why the other person has stopped communicating. It is also detrimental to the "ghoster" because, often, they don't have the courage or emotional maturity to communicate their boundaries in a healthy way and may just repeat the pattern without ever facing their fear of conflict or having the courage to express themselves. Those that live in integrity with themselves communicate their boundaries clearly prior to withdrawing their energy from a relationship.

ENERGETIC BOUNDARIES

Energetic boundaries relate to the protection and awareness of your energy field. It is important to protect your energy field. Some people are more sensitive to energy than others. If you are energy sensitive or empathic to the energies of others, it is essential to establish boundaries to protect your energy and prevent energy drain or emotional overwhelm. One way to know if you are energy sensitive is to ask yourself what happens when you walk into a room. Do you pick up on how others are feeling? Is your energy impacted by the energy in the room?

Here are some key points about energetic boundaries:

Consciously manage your energy flow: Be mindful of who and where you give your energy to. Awareness of how you feel in the presence of others is critical in knowing if a relationship is healthy for you or not. Ensure that you do not consistently surround yourself with people who sap your energy.

For example, you are around someone who is always stressed and has drama and chaos in their life; when you are around them, you also feel stressed and chaotic. You may need to set an energetic boundary by becoming aware of this feeling and acknowledging it as theirs, not yours! You can still be supportive and empathic without taking on the drama and chaos of their life.

Protect your energy field: Visualizations like "zipping up" can be effective tools for creating an energetic shield around yourself. Imagine a protective bubble or visualize energy flowing in a specific direction to help maintain boundaries. To zip up your energy, close your eyes and imagine that you have a zipper in front of you starting at the base of your spine that goes up and over your right shoulder. Picture zipping yourself up and, therefore, creating an energetic boundary between yourself and the world around you.

Discerning energetic interactions: Be selective about the people and environments you engage with to help preserve energy and prevent negative influences from affecting your wellbeing. An energy drain can feel like you have depleted your energy tank, and you may be left feeling the emotions of the person you were interacting with. Some people leave you feeling like you've been run over by a truck or irritated by the conversation despite having been happy before the encounter. Sometimes energy drains can be less obvious; for example, when I am around people that I love, I automatically want to take care of them, serve them, and contribute to them. It is a natural part of who I am. If I do not consciously take time to fill myself up, I end up feeling drained and depleted. Sometimes this can lead to resentment. Therefore, it is essential to have time alone to fill up your energy reserves. Regardless of whether intentional or not, by just being around people, you may unconsciously be giving away your energy.

Physical Boundaries

Physical boundaries involve setting limits on how others can interact with your personal space and with your body itself. Knowing, communicating, and respecting your physical boundaries is crucial for maintaining a sense of autonomy and safety.

Regarding your personal space, define and be aware of your physical boundaries in social situations. Establish boundaries that respect your personal space, such as adequate physical distance and not receiving touch without permission.

Setting intimate boundaries around your body also is crucial for maintaining healthy relationships and ensuring that both parties feel respected and safe. Here are some steps to help you communicate your intimacy boundaries effectively:

Self awareness: Before you can communicate your boundaries to someone else, it's important to be aware of your own needs, desires, and limits regarding intimate interactions. Take some time to reflect on what feels good and comfortable for you, and note areas of your body that you may not want to be touched. If you are unfamiliar with your own body and what feels good, participating in a KunYin® class can support you to connect more deeply with your body, your emotions, and what feels good for you. To participate in a KunYin® class either in person or online, visit kunyin.com.au and try it out for *free*!

Reflect on past experiences: Reflect on any past experiences that have made you feel uncomfortable in intimate situations. Understanding these can help you identify your boundaries and communicate them more effectively.

Communicate openly and honestly: When discussing your intimacy boundaries with a partner, it's important to be open and honest about your needs and desires. Clearly communicate what you are comfortable with and what you are not comfortable with, and be willing to listen to your partner's boundaries as well.

Use "I" statements: When communicating your boundaries, use "I" statements to express your feelings and needs. For example, instead of saying "You always make me feel uncomfortable," say "I feel uncomfortable when . . . "

Respect yourself: Remember that it's okay to set boundaries and prioritize your own needs and wellbeing. Your body will let you know if it is feeling uncomfortable. Bringing awareness to where you may feel tension, uneasiness, or holding your breath can be signs that your body is not feeling safe with the boundaries you are setting. Remember, you have the right to say no to any intimate interactions that make you feel uncomfortable or unsafe.

Monitor and adjust: As your needs and boundaries may change over time, it's important to regularly check in with yourself and your partner to ensure that your boundaries are being respected. Be open to adjusting your boundaries as needed.

By communicating your intimacy boundaries effectively, you can create a foundation of trust, respect, and safety in your relationships, leading to healthier and more fulfilling connections.

Mental Boundaries

Mental boundaries involve protecting your mind and psychological wellbeing by controlling the information and influences that enter your thoughts. Maintaining mental boundaries is essential for promoting mental clarity and emotional balance. Here are key points about mental boundaries:

Stand guard at the entrance to your mind: Be mindful of the content and sources of information that you expose yourself to. Limit viewing of any content or information that may create fear or stress or disturb you, like television, for example. What you see filters into your subconscious mind. According to Bruce Lipton, the subconscious mind processes some twenty million environmental stimuli per second versus the forty environmental stimuli interpreted by the conscious mind in the same second. By consciously choosing what you allow into your mind, you can prevent negative influences and promote positive thinking.

Be selective: Choosing to engage with ideas, beliefs, and conversations that align with your values and goals supports your mental wellbeing and personal growth. Establishing boundaries around the type and amount of information you consume, such as news, social media, newspapers, and television can help you maintain mental clarity and focus.

Choose your peers wisely: It is human nature to want to be accepted and be part of your communities in order to receive a sense of belonging and connection. If your mental boundaries are not strong, it is easy to take on the beliefs of your peers. What do they believe, practice, and how do they behave? Are their behaviors in alignment with yours?

If you are new to setting mental boundaries, start by going through your social media feeds and unfollow anyone who posts things that are disturbing or not in alignment with your beliefs. Limit the time you spend watching the news or any other medium that can evoke a sense of fear. I am not saying you should be ignorant to what is happening in the world, but I am saying be critical of what you are consuming. Do not tolerate any name calling or being spoken to in a way that is undignified or disrespectful even if sometimes these words or names are said in jest. Your subconscious doesn't know the difference between what is real and what is not. Be aware of accepting these types of behaviors, especially from people that you love and care about.

EMOTIONAL BOUNDARIES
Emotional boundaries involve recognizing and honoring your feelings, needs, and limits in your relationships and interactions with others. Establishing emotional boundaries is crucial for self care, emotional wellbeing, and maintaining healthy connections.

Self awareness and self validation: Recognizing and validating your emotions is essential for setting healthy emotional boundaries. This involves understanding your feelings and needs and communicating them effectively. In my experience, the more at home I am with my own emotions, such as sadness and anger, the easier it is for me to be present with others as they are moving through theirs. My clients that are triggered by others' emotions are often not okay with expressing those same emotions themselves. KunYin® has been an incredible tool that I use to identify, move through, and own all the emotions that I feel in a healthy way.

Respecting emotional limits: Communicating boundaries around how you expect to be treated emotionally, such as avoiding criticism, manipulation, or disrespect, is vital for maintaining emotional health and self respect.

Healthy relationship dynamics: Establishing boundaries in relationships, where you make it clear what you will and will not tolerate and your partner does the same, helps create a supportive and respectful environment where you feel valued, understood, and emotionally secure.

By understanding and implementing boundaries in these four areas—energetic, physical, mental, and emotional—you can cultivate a greater sense of self awareness, self respect, and overall wellbeing in your social interactions. Setting and maintaining boundaries is a continuous process that requires self reflection, communication, and a commitment to personal growth.

By honoring and respecting yourself, you cultivate a sense of empowerment and maintain fulfilling connections with the people you love. Remember that setting boundaries is an act of self love and self respect.

Masculine and Feminine Principles

As humanity evolves, particularly in the last few decades, there has been an increase of women stepping into their divine feminine. This is critical to reclaiming the lost and diminished aspects of being empowered in the feminine parts of yourself. It's not only women who need to connect with these parts. So many men and young boys are disconnected from the feminine qualities of deep emotional connection, intuition, and creativity—aspects that have traditionally, through patriarchal views, been seen as weak. This suppression of emotions has been tragic. According to statistics reported in 2022, males are three times more likely to take their own life than females. As a woman and leader in your family and community, you have the power to lead the way for all people to support more open expression of emotions and safety and intimacy in relationships. But you must do the work first before you can authentically lead the way.

The feminine principle is inherently designed to create, to give birth to new ideas, concepts, and revolutionary ways in which to live in the world, and the masculine is to provide the support and structure for it to come to fruition. I believe that the next wave of evolution as a species to grow in consciousness is not only the reclamation of the divine feminine but the integration, healing, and embodiment of the divine masculine *and* feminine within everyone.

The concepts of masculine and feminine principles symbolize certain qualities traditionally associated with masculinity and femininity. They are not gender based but, rather, founded on the philosophy that every person, male and female, has these two polarities within. To live in balance, harmony, and oneness, it is imperative that you cultivate a healthy balance between these two energies.

Healing the unhealthy aspects of your identity and creating new and empowering beliefs and ways of being will support coming into wholeness and oneness with yourself and, therefore, the world in which you operate.

Masculine Principles

Right side of body / left brain: The right side of the body (masculine) is controlled by the left hemisphere of the brain, which is considered the analytical and logical side, the one responsible for tasks such as language processing, reasoning, and mathematical computations. In the context of the masculine principle, this alignment signifies a focus on logic, reason, and analytical thinking, which are traditionally associated with masculine energy.

Shiva: In Hindu tradition, Shiva represents the masculine aspect of the divine, embodying qualities such as destruction, transformation, and regeneration. Shiva symbolizes masculine energy that is powerful, transcendent, and associated with action and creation.

Yang: In Chinese philosophy, yang represents the active, assertive, and outwardly focused energy that is associated with masculinity. Yang qualities include strength, assertiveness, and dynamism.

Bones and skeleton: Bones and the skeletal structure represent strength, support, and stability. In the context of the masculine principle, bones and the skeleton symbolize the structural, foundational aspects of masculinity, emphasizing qualities like resilience, endurance, and solidity.

Mental: Masculine energy is often associated with the mental realm, emphasizing qualities such as logic, reason, and analytical thinking. This mental focus reflects the masculine principle of being rational, strategic, and intellectually driven.

Action: Masculine energy is characterized by a proactive approach to life, emphasizing action, decision making, and goal-oriented behavior. The principle of action aligns with masculinity's focus on assertiveness, determination, and forward momentum.

Determined: Masculine energy is often depicted as resolute, persistent, and unwavering in the pursuit of goals. Being determined is a key aspect of the masculine principle, reflecting qualities like drive, ambition, and perseverance.

Single focus: Masculine energy tends to exhibit a singular, focused approach to tasks and goals, emphasizing concentration, efficiency, and goal-directed behavior. The principle of single focus reflects masculinity's emphasis on clarity, purpose, and directed energy.

Structural: Masculine energy is often associated with structure, organization, and order. Structure in the masculine principle highlights qualities such as discipline, stability, and a methodical approach to tasks and responsibilities.

Linear: Masculine energy often follows a linear, step-by-step progression in thinking and action. The concept of linearity in the masculine principle emphasizes logical reasoning, sequential processing, and a direct approach to problem solving and decision making.

External: Masculine energy is often directed outward, focusing on external goals, achievements, and interactions with the outside world. Externality in the masculine principle emphasizes engagement with the external environment, assertiveness, and action-oriented behavior.

Giving: Masculine energy can be expressed through acts of service, generosity, and providing support to others. Giving, in the context of the masculine principle, reflects qualities such as protection, provision, and care for others.

Doing: Masculine energy is often associated with doing, taking action, and achieving results through active engagement with tasks and goals. The concept of doing in the masculine principle underscores qualities such as productivity, initiative, and effectiveness.

Demonstrative knowing: Masculine energy tends to rely on demonstrative knowing, which involves tangible evidence, observable facts, and explicit demonstrations of knowledge. This approach aligns with the masculine principle's emphasis on reason, logic, and concrete understanding.

Reason: Masculine energy values reason, logic, and rational thinking as essential tools for problem solving, decision making, and understanding the world. Reason in the masculine principle underscores the importance of critical thinking, analysis, and sound judgment.

Specificity: Masculine energy often seeks specificity, clarity, and precision in communication, tasks, and goals. The principle of specificity highlights masculinity's focus on details, accuracy, and exactness in addressing challenges and pursuing objectives.

Feminine Principles

Left side of the body / right brain: The right brain is often associated with creativity, intuition, holistic thinking, and emotional processing and controls the left side (feminine) of the body. These qualities align with the feminine principle, which values creativity, intuition, emotional intelligence, and the ability to see the interconnectedness of all things. The right brain's capacity for creativity and intuition reflects the feminine energy's nurturing and empathetic nature.

Shakti: In Hinduism, Shakti is the divine feminine energy, representing power, creativity, and transformation. It embodies the qualities of strength, creativity, and dynamic energy. Shakti is often associated with fertility, abundance, and the creative force of the Universe. It symbolizes the power of creation, nurturing, and transformation, all of which are central to the feminine principle.

Yin: Yin energy is receptive, intuitive, and nurturing. It embodies qualities such as gentleness, intuition, and interconnectedness, aligning with the feminine principle of balance and harmony. Yin energy is associated with qualities like introspection, empathy, and emotional depth, reflecting the feminine energy's focus on nurturing, intuition, and interconnectedness.

Muscles, discs, and tissue: These physical components of the body symbolize strength, support, and flexibility, reflecting the nurturing and supportive aspect of the feminine principle. Muscles provide strength and stability, while tissues and discs support and protect the body's structures. These elements mirror the feminine energy's capacity for nurturing, supporting, and providing a stable foundation for growth and transformation.

Emotional: Emotions are often associated with the feminine principle, emphasizing sensitivity, empathy, and emotional intelligence. The ability to feel deeply, empathize with others, and express emotions authentically is a key aspect of the feminine energy. Embracing and understanding emotions is central to the feminine principle, as it fosters connection, empathy, and authenticity in relationships.

Reaction: The ability to respond to stimuli quickly and intuitively can be seen as a reflection of the feminine principle's dynamic and responsive nature. Reacting with sensitivity, empathy, and creativity allows the feminine energy to adapt to changing circumstances, nurture relationships, and foster growth and transformation.

Creative: Creativity is a hallmark of the feminine principle, representing the ability to generate new ideas, solutions, and expressions. Creativity allows the feminine energy to innovate, nurture, and transform, encouraging growth and evolution in both individuals and communities. Creative expression is a powerful tool for connecting with others, fostering empathy, and promoting collaboration.

Diffuse awareness: The concept of diffuse awareness comes from the teachings of Alison Armstrong, an educator in relationship dynamics. She teaches that a feminine trait is to have a natural capacity for what she calls "diffuse awareness," meaning that women can often be aware of multiple things at once, including emotions, relationships, details, and nuances in their environment. This ability allows women to be highly intuitive, empathetic, and sensitive to subtle cues and changes in their surroundings compared to their masculine counterparts.

Flexible: Flexibility symbolizes adaptability, openness, and fluidity, which are qualities aligned with the feminine principle's ability to adjust and flow with change. Flexibility allows the feminine energy to embrace uncertainty, navigate challenges, and find creative solutions to complex problems. Adapting with grace and resilience is a key aspect of the feminine principle, enabling growth, transformation, and evolution.

Nonlinear (curve): In addition to the natural more curvaceous shape of the feminine body, nonlinear thinking and curved paths represent a more intuitive and creative approach to problem solving, reflecting the feminine principle's embrace of complexity and interconnectedness. Nonlinear thinking allows the feminine energy to see patterns, connections, and possibilities. Embracing curved paths and nonlinear approaches fosters creativity, innovation, and unique perspectives.

Internal: The internal focus highlights introspection, intuition, and emotional depth, qualities often associated with the feminine principle. Internal reflection allows the feminine energy to deepen its understanding of self and others, fostering empathy, intuition, and emotional intelligence.

By turning inward, the feminine energy can cultivate self awareness, emotional resilience, and a deep connection to its inner wisdom.

Receiving: The ability to receive and be open to new ideas, experiences, and energies reflects the receptive nature of the feminine principle. Receiving with openness and receptivity allows the feminine energy to nurture relationships, foster collaboration, and embrace new possibilities. Being open to receiving allows the feminine energy to connect deeply with others, feel the fullness of love and other experiences, cultivate empathy, and foster growth and transformation.

Being: The concept of "being" emphasizes presence, mindfulness, and connection to one's inner self, aligning with the feminine principle's focus on intuition and introspection. Being in the present moment allows the feminine energy to connect deeply with its emotions, intuition, and inner wisdom.

Intuition: Intuition embodies the essence of the feminine principle, signifying a profound understanding or insight that surpasses logic and reasoning. Valued for its capacity to unveil truths, spark creativity, and guide decision making, intuitive guidance stems from a profound connection with oneself and one's body.

In summary, every person has both of these energies within them, as well as the ability to express the qualities of masculine and feminine energies. Energy is not isolated to a particular gender; however, depending on your conditioning, discussed further in the next chapter, you may be inclined to embody one energy more than the other. Yet, to experience the fullness and harmony within, you must learn to bring balance to both. This is key in living the sovereign woman's way.

Responsibility

A foundational principle of this book is that you *must*, and I repeat *must*, take responsibility for your life. You are responsible for how you feel, act, and behave. You must understand that you are at the center of your life's experience. There is no one to blame, no one to shame, no one to judge. This doesn't mean that you blame, shame, and judge yourself, no. I define responsibility as being response-able and able to respond. At all times, you are able to respond to situations and circumstances and make your choices even if sometimes you feel they are out of your hands. You are responsible for bringing awareness to your triggers, your healing, your emotions, and identifying and changing your beliefs if they do not serve you in the highest and best way.

If you are still reading, thank you! If you are triggered and still reading, thank you even more! It means that you are not afraid of the tough conversations and that you are ready to move on to the next chapters.

## CHAPTER 2

The Creation of Identity

Throughout your lifetime, across your genetics, within your culture, and in the places you experience life and mature, your identity is shaped. These systems define who you are or, rather, who you perceive yourself to be. Often much of this identity is formed by the subconscious mind without your conscious awareness. For the most part, you haven't actively created your identity. Instead, you have unknowingly absorbed and created beliefs and recurring behavioral patterns, which I refer to as programs. These programs operate constantly, influencing your actions without your conscious realization. You mistake these programs for yourself, but they are not you. They form a part of your conditioning as shaped by your environment, society, culture, religion, family, and peers. Understanding this conditioning is crucial. You have been conditioned to behave in ways based on what is deemed acceptable or tolerable. Once you recognize these patterns as programs you are running, you gain the power to choose whether to continue running them or not.

Who Are You?

So who are you then? Are you who you think you are? If your subconscious stores your beliefs, and your beliefs run your behavior, and you don't know what your beliefs are . . . Did you even consciously create *you*? I don't believe so. Until the unseen becomes seen, you are running programs that you didn't even know you had.

I'm not suggesting that there is something wrong with you; many of the programs that you created have served you. They have helped you survive; kept you strong, resilient, and knowledgeable; and helped you feel loved and accepted. However, you will never really experience your true self until you become aware of these unseen programs that you have been running. Once you see them, you can either consciously choose to change them or stay the same. Neither is right nor wrong; it depends on the situation and the particular program. The point is intention: Becoming aware and choosing is how you become free. I likened the unveiling of my programs to being in a self imposed cage that I didn't know I was in. It was a golden cage because these programs had served me and brought me much success in life. However, it was still a cage. Once I recognized the subconscious programming I was running, it was like the cage vanished, and I was finally free to choose. It wasn't my fault or my parents' fault; it is the human default and a necessary part of my growth on Earth as a soul in a physical body. It was my conditioning.

How did you become the woman that you are today? Have you ever really stopped to consider this question?

Even before birth, you began absorbing the emotions and experiences of your mother while you were in her womb. These early influences, along with everything you have encountered in your life, are stored in your cellular memory. Remember what I said about energy? These vibrations of energy, the protons, neutrons, and the essence of your experiences are carried within you from the beginning, shaping your beliefs and perceptions as you grow.

According to Tony Robbins, America's top life and business strategist, the two greatest fears that all humans share are the fear of not being enough and the fear of not being loved. Regardless of how confident you are or who you are, every single person harbors these two fears. Since the loss of love is one of our greatest anxieties, you need to ask yourself this question: "Who did I need to be in order to be loved by my mother and father?" As the primary source of your survival as a child, you needed their love and care—regardless of whether it was abundant or lacking—in order to thrive. This necessity laid the foundation that created and shaped the identity you believed you needed to receive love. For me to receive the love I wanted from my mother, I felt I had to be a good girl; I needed to do what I was told, be nice, help around the house, and refrain from answering back, being cheeky, or making too much noise, especially when the news was on in the evenings! To earn my father's love, I believed I needed to be strong, smart, and independent.

Your upbringing, experiences, friends, and culture all play a role in creating the ways you believe you "should" be. Remember, from birth to seven years old, you absorb everything in your environment. Reflecting on my own childhood, I recall several moments that shaped how I viewed myself and who I needed to be in order to be loved. It was those moments that influenced how I saw myself, how I interacted with others, and, ultimately, the woman that I became.

One of those moments was at age five. Don't ask me why I said what I said, but, one day, playing in the school yard with my friend Fiona, I turned to her and said, "Mrs. Joseph has big boobs!" Mrs. Joseph was our prep teacher. The look of shock on Fiona's face at the word "boobs" caused a wave of fear and shame to rush over me. My friend said that she would tell the teacher what I had said. I was petrified. I didn't want to get into trouble. I felt a wave of terror go over my body and felt sick to my stomach. I had been taught that I needed to be a "good girl" and talking about the teacher's breasts would not have been considered something that I should be talking about! I went home that night and told my mum that I didn't want to go to school tomorrow because I was sick. She said that I should stop being so ridiculous and that by tomorrow I would be feeling better. My plan didn't work! I had to come up with another one! In my little creative five-year-old mind, I decided that if I started being nice to this friend, then maybe I could get out of trouble. Low and behold, it worked! This led me to believe that being nice to others was the key to love and acceptance and a way to avoid being rejected or shamed. I had to be a good girl and be nice to everyone. This early experience, along with the beliefs ingrained in me by my parents, planted the seeds of people-pleasing behavior that persisted throughout my life.

As I grew older, this pattern of prioritizing others' needs over my own became ingrained in my relationships, leaving me feeling empty and disconnected from my own desires and, ultimately, my own identity. The habit of pleasing people had overshadowed my ability to identify and prioritize my own needs and wants. It was a coping mechanism that originated from that pivotal moment in my childhood and which continued to shape my interactions with others as an adult.

It wasn't until I was in my late thirties attending a retreat and was asked to choose a song that I would like to dance to that I realized . . . I didn't even know what I liked. I observed my mind racing, trying to find the perfect song . . . a song that others would like, one that no one else had chosen, one that would make me look good. I had absolutely no clue as to what I liked if I didn't have to consider anyone else's needs, desires, or feelings. I didn't even know what mine were. Now when I look back, I can't believe that I am the same person. I have healed and transformed so many aspects of myself.

Consider this question: Who would you be if there were no expectations of you?

Reflecting on your own journey, consider the significant moments and memories from your early years, from birth to seven. What beliefs and behaviors were ingrained in you during this formative period? Who did you have to be to be loved by your mother? Who did you have to be to be loved by your father? How did you learn to navigate the world and seek acceptance and love?

From the ages of seven to fourteen, life is all about finding purpose through your experiences. You build on the identity that you created from birth to seven, and throughout your life, particularly up to twenty-one, you strengthen your identity based on your experiences.

I still remember being seven or eight years old and sitting outside a doctor's consultation room, somehow aware of my mother's struggles with depression after the loss of her beloved father. I felt a deep sense of helplessness and sadness. I told myself that I needed to have it all handled and take care of my own needs so that she didn't have to worry about me. It was weak to ask for help or to show my emotions, so, in response to this perceived need to be strong, independent, and hide my own emotions so I could support my mum, I learned to put my own needs aside and adopt a facade of bravery—to protect myself from vulnerability and to support my mother in her time of need.

During this critical period of childhood, you often develop coping mechanisms and behaviors to navigate challenging situations and emotions.

- ♡ What memories and feelings stand out for you from the ages of seven to fourteen?
- ♡ How did you learn to cope and adapt to the circumstances around you during this time?

Consider these reflections as you explore the ways in which your early experiences have shaped the person you are today.

When I was nineteen, I met my first love. I was very young and had little experience in relationships, but I was entirely committed to him. After three months of dating, he told me that he had been with two other women during the time we had been together. I was devastated; I felt as though my heart was breaking into pieces. I had never experienced heartbreak before, so I had no idea what it felt like, but it felt as though my heart was quite literally breaking. I asked my aunty, "What can I do to help a broken heart?" She just looked blankly at me and held me as I cried in her arms. Being vulnerable was not comfortable for me, and I did not like how exposed it made me feel. I considered it weak, and crying was not something that I usually allowed myself to do. In fact, I would do almost anything to avoid the feeling of sadness. So, once again, my identity came to my rescue, and I decided that I would love and forgive him, but I would never again give all of myself in a relationship. I would give ninety-five percent of myself, but the last five percent was just for me, and in that way, I believed I would never be able to get hurt again. The mix of beliefs and emotions had me stay in that relationship despite feeling betrayed; however, as I was only willing to give ninety-five percent of myself, I was not truly able to trust and allow for deep heart opening, intimacy, and connection.

During this critical period of adolescence through to adulthood, you develop coping mechanisms and beliefs and behaviors to navigate love, relationships, and challenging situations and emotions.

- ♡ What memories and feelings stand out for you from the ages of fourteen to twenty-one?
- ♡ How did you learn to cope and adapt to the circumstances around you during this time?

Consider these reflections as you explore the ways in which your early experiences have shaped the person you are today.

What I have seen in over a decade of working with thousands of people is that in response to this unconsciously created identity, people have a tendency to swing back and forth, like a pendulum, as their ways of being were often created in response to a need for survival. When your survival identity reaches a threshold, it often swings in the opposite direction. I will give you an example from my life. As I have shared throughout the book, I created a people-pleaser identity as the woman that would bend over backwards for people, put everyone else's needs before her own, would say yes when she really meant no, and was often left feeling overwhelmed, tired, disappointed, unappreciated, sad, and confused. This led to a swing in the opposite direction toward an identity that was created as a reaction. This woman was angry, outspoken, easily frustrated, and withdrawn. Being only five-foot-nothing, my mum would refer to me as an angry little ant! When I was done being angry, I would swing back to the people-pleaser. Until I hit the survival identity threshold and then back I swung to the angry little ant. And so it would continue.

Another example is that of one of my clients who loved and craved attention from her father. When she was a child, her mum was busy taking care of a newborn and didn't have the time to give her the love and attention that she wanted. So she would go and seek this love from her father. He, a gruff, Italian man, who was usually not affectionate, would give her a hug, and then push her away and say, "Go! Be off with you. Get outta here." From a young age, she chased the affection of men who were emotionally unavailable. When they pushed her away, she would keep coming back in spite of being treated poorly because that was the example of how love was shown to her by the first man that she ever loved. If a man genuinely showed her love that she didn't have to chase, she didn't want it. It felt unfamiliar, unsafe, and uncomfortable, so she would push it away.

And so the pendulum would swing between wanting love by chasing it and then, when getting it easily, pushing it away—back and forth. This pattern stopped her from being able to create lasting healthy relationships and attracting emotionally available partners.

You too have many ways of being that you have created in order to survive and thrive in this world. To delve deeper into the creation of your identity, you can download the Creation of Identity worksheet and discover more at thesovereignwomansway.com.

The Pendulum Effect

The pendulum effect is a phenomenon that I identified to explain the polarization of certain behaviors. It is a powerful observation that can change the way you operate forever. The pendulum effect occurs as you grow and become more aware of your conditioning and the beliefs that shape your life. Remember, you construct patterns and identities to navigate the world and ensure your survival. However, as you become increasingly conscious of these aspects, you may find yourself swinging to the opposite extreme in an effort to create change.

This swing can happen in a positive way, like when you experience a breakthrough moment when doing inner work. In such a breakthrough, you gain deep insights that bring your unconscious into your awareness, prompting you to take decisive action and make significant changes in your life. The pendulum swings dramatically the other way, and you see results and positive transformations unfold right in front of your eyes.

Yet, as you immerse yourself in this new way of being, particularly if you are consistently on a growth path, you may eventually encounter limitations and unproductive aspects of the new behavior. Every pattern or behavior serves you until it no longer does. The key to understanding its utility lies in your awareness. Without awareness, you operate on

THE PENDULUM
Effect

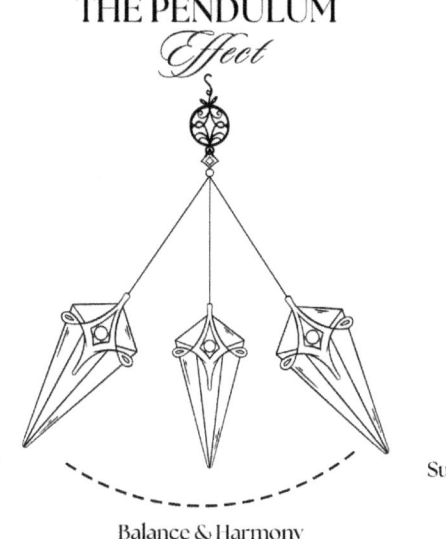

Reaction to Survival Self   Survival Self

Balance & Harmony

autopilot, trapped within the framework of your conditioning. This can be prevalent when healing the rebellious or compliant teenager identities that are created from the ages of seven to fourteen and fourteen to twenty-one.

Many of you reading this may relate to operating on autopilot, unaware of the conscious choices you can make about how you show up in the world. The pendulum goes from one extreme to the other, causing you to swing back and forth.

The crucial realization is that sustainable change cannot be built on reactions. Awareness is the compass that guides you in navigating the pendulum effect and finding a balanced way of being that truly serves you in the long run.

When I came back from my trip to the United Kingdom in 2022, I had gone from experiencing the highest of the highs, of bliss and joy, to experiencing the complete opposite. What goes up must come down. I had never before felt such depths of sadness and loss. I remember being in my sacred space, crying, asking the Creator, "Why do I have to feel this? Why does it have to be so painful and hard?" The Creator replied, "I wanted you to experience the full spectrum of what it is to be a human being. How can you know the light without experiencing the dark? How can you know joy without experiencing pain?" I was being stretched so that I could experience more of what it is to be alive, to be human. To have a deeper sense of love and compassion for those who were in pain and suffering. I was also learning to heal wounds that had never been present to me before.

I didn't know this at the time, but I was being led to a place of balance, to learn how to balance these polarizing emotions and to live consciously in a beautiful state of harmony.

Conditioning

Only when you bring awareness to your subconscious beliefs and programming can you truly create the person you want to become. You must acknowledge the decisions you have made (yes, you may have made them consciously or unconsciously, but you definitely made them). This is not about putting the blame on your parents, siblings, friends, family, or ancestors. This is about taking full responsibility for your life because you have been given the gift of free will. You made these choices so that you could survive and thrive in the world. And now that you know this, you can consciously decide whether to continue following them or break free from their influence. Once you know better, you must do better if you want to be the sovereign woman you were born to be!

Some of these beliefs and patterns may have served you well in the past, bringing you to where you are now. However, there may come a point, perhaps even now, where these patterns no longer serve your growth and evolution.

To progress to the next level of love, passion, and fulfillment in your life, and to deepen your experience of love and connection with yourself, you need to release these outdated patterns and create new ones that empower you.

Letting go of the old is essential to make way for the next version of you. Think of it as a cup of coffee that's already full to the brim. There is no space for more. It's time to let go, to pour out what is no longer needed to create space for the new ways of being. Letting go of these ingrained patterns and outdated belief systems is not always easy; it will require effort. When you consider how long some of these beliefs have been around and how they have been strengthened over the decades, you can appreciate why it's a process that demands commitment and courage.

This journey of transformation has brought you to what comes next: The willingness to release attachments. To move forward, you must shed the identity you have constructed for yourself. This involves letting go of who you think you are or who you believe yourself to be so that you can become the woman that you were born to be. These ways of being have served you, they have allowed you to achieve the results that you have attained thus far. However, to evolve, you have to let go of what no longer serves you to make space for the new. You cannot be attached to who you think you are; you will need to become masterful at the art of nonattachment, which I discuss further in Chapter 7. Nonattachment is exactly what it says: Not being attached to the old versions of you, to people's opinions of you, to the structures and beliefs that you have created from survival. Rather, consciously create who you choose to be so that you can live life fully on your terms, free to express and be your true self.

The Thinking-Feeling Feedback Loop

The thinking-feeling feedback loop is another system that I discovered as I journeyed through creating lasting change in my own life. The thinking-feeling feedback loop demonstrates the intricate interactions between your mind, body, and soul, as shown in the following diagram.

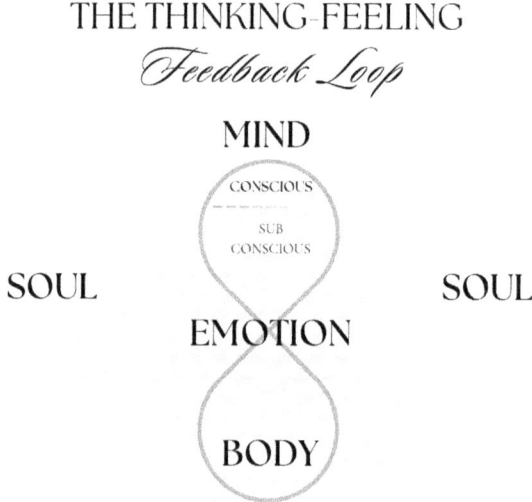

THE THINKING-FEELING
Feedback Loop

MIND

CONSCIOUS

SUB
CONSCIOUS

SOUL   SOUL

EMOTION

BODY

To break it down, think of your brain as the command center of your body, like built-in hardware, a control panel if you will. It's a complex organ made up of billions of nerve cells called neurons that help you process information, make decisions, and control your body's functions. When you touch something hot, for example, your brain sends signals to you to move your hand away to protect you from harm. It's like the supercomputer that runs the show behind the scenes, making sure everything in your body works together smoothly.

Your brain is hardwired to keep you alive. Its primary function is survival rather than things like happiness, pleasure, or joy that contribute to a fulfilling existence.

Now let's talk about the mind. Imagine your mind as the collection of your thoughts, emotions, memories, and consciousness. It's like the software that runs on the brain's hardware. Your mind is what makes you unique and shapes your personality, beliefs, and experiences. It's where your creativity, imagination, and dreams come from. While the brain is physical and can be studied through science and technology, the mind is more abstract and mysterious because it's not something you can see or touch directly.

Contained within the mind are both the subconscious and conscious realms. The subconscious mind, housing primal survival instincts, operates silently, absorbing information from your surroundings without your active involvement or awareness.

Throughout the journey of life, each experience, thought, memory, and belief system is stored within the depths of your subconscious mind. Often the contents of your subconscious remain hidden until a particular conversation or experience triggers them and draws them to the surface of your consciousness. For example, the discussions, questions, or journaling prompts in this book may pose thought-provoking questions and guide you through transformative meditations to uncover the hidden treasures of your subconscious mind.

The beliefs that reside within your subconscious shape your thoughts, emotions, and behaviors and, ultimately, influence the outcomes of your decisions and the relationships in your life. The more you are aware of those subconscious beliefs, the more they will rise to the consciousness, and the more power you will have to change them.

For example, you may have grown up seeing your parents remain in a marriage even though they were unhappy and go through their lives sad and resentful, never experiencing the joy and pleasure that comes from a happy and fulfilling relationship.

Not having grown up with healthy family dynamics, you may believe that that is just how relationships are. Conversely, if you saw a healthy relationship modeled, you may believe that you will never stay in an unhappy marriage. You will choose how you want to respond to life based on your experiences and subsequent beliefs because you have your own unique experiences and your soul has its own unique lessons and purpose in being. Once the beliefs that have been created are brought into the conscious mind, you have the free will to choose how you will respond. Prior to conscious awareness, your "hardwired program" will run until it is exposed.

By bridging the gap between the subconscious and conscious realms, you gain the ability to intentionally make changes. Without this awareness, your body and mind respond instinctively to these deeply ingrained beliefs, shaping your experiences and reactions on a subconscious level and effectively creating your reality.

I had an experience as a seven-year-old child where I was feeling safe and secure in my bed but was touched in places on my body that made me feel uncomfortable. It was shocking to me, and I was not sure how to process that feeling. It felt good and wrong at the same time. It was confusing for my mind and shocking to my body. In adulthood, this has manifested in subconscious reactions from my body when I am unprepared or taken by surprise. This impacted my intimate relationships and feelings of safety and security in my body as an adult until my late thirties. As your body is the history book of everything you have ever experienced, it retains the memories and sensations of past encounters, particularly strong ones that leave an imprint on you, influencing your present reactions and emotions until you have had the opportunity to fully experience and move through them, releasing them from your cellular memory.

Subconscious beliefs that I created included:

- My body is shameful.
- I am afraid of intimacy.
- Pleasure is wrong.

It wasn't until I started to move my body and really connect to my erotic nature through movement that I was able to not only clear these beliefs from my consciousness, but break the patterns of shame and judgment of pleasure, sex, and intimacy.

Over the years as a psychosomatic therapist, I have witnessed many women who, when going through adolescence and becoming women and growing womanly, curvy hips and breasts, were picked on or shamed as they developed. Feeling embarrassed, they fell into a pattern of slumping over or rolling their shoulders forward to hide their breasts, consequently closing down their hearts and their feminine expression.

To disrupt this recurring cycle, it is essential to approach your inner workings holistically, addressing all facets of your being. While you may intellectually understand that you are safe, true transformation occurs when your body experiences safety and is free to express itself. This can lead to a profound shift in conditioned responses and a resetting and calming of the nervous system.

The key to lasting change lies in acknowledging and resolving this thinking-feeling feedback loop and actively moving the energy through the physical body. It is through the combination of movement of the body, undoing its ingrained patterns, and identifying and clearing limiting beliefs from the mind that you can create profound and lasting transformations, paving the way for a more empowered and authentic way of being.

KunYin®, the unique movement modality that I developed, offers a transformative approach to supporting the body, mind, and soul in processing and moving energy and emotions throughout the body. Through this practice, you can break the patterns that keep you shut down or closed off and reprogram yourself at a cellular level, fostering a deep sense of safety, love, and empowerment and allowing emotions to flow freely and healthily through you.

If you are intrigued by the KunYin® practice and its potential to facilitate inner transformation, I warmly invite you to embark on a seven-day complimentary trial of the portal. This online space is dedicated to feminine embodiment, providing a nurturing environment for women to explore and cultivate a healthy relationship with their body, energy, and emotions.

Living in a Beautiful State

I'd like to share something I learned during my time in India from the teachings of the incredible Krishnaji and Preethaji, transformational leaders and the co-founders of the Oneness Movement, a global initiative aimed at awakening individual consciousness and cultivating a sense of oneness in humanity. Preethaji spoke of two states in which one can live: A beautiful state or a suffering state. Initially, I was unsure if I believed this, but as I delved deeper, I began to see that every way of being falls into one of these two categories. There are different levels of beautiful states, from feeling blissful or ecstatic to being content and at peace, and all are considered beautiful states of connection. Similarly, suffering can be experienced as anxiety, fear, loneliness, hurt, anger, or frustration—any state in which you are separate from yourself, others, and your Creator.

It is important that you are able to dissolve that suffering state, and when it arises for you, to instead cultivate a beautiful state. And in that beautiful, harmonious state, you are not separate, you are not alienated. Rather, you expand to include others, and your experience of life and yourself is one of connection.

What I have also come to understand through the Law of Attraction (the principle that your thoughts, intentions, and state of being manifest your reality, drawing positive or negative experiences into your life) is that creating from a state of suffering leads to limited results in your life. If you are creating from a state of suffering or negativity, you may attract more experiences that resonate with that energy, which limits the positive results you can produce. If you create from a beautiful state, the results that you gain will be in resonance with that energy!

Many people have built businesses and relationships from a place of suffering, whether to escape the suffering or to fill a void created by a lack of love. Until your unconscious patterns become conscious, you will continue to operate from a place of suffering. Understanding your ways of being is key. By recognizing how you became the person you are today and where you fall on the spectrum of beauty and suffering, you can break free from cycles that prevent you from experiencing true fulfillment, joy, peace, and balance in your life.

Bringing the unconscious to the conscious gives you the power to choose to create from a beautiful state. Even if you might be living from a place of results created by suffering, you can heal and choose to create from a beautiful state.

The shift in awareness from suffering to beautiful states will open you up to the realization that you have the opportunity to live a life of connection and abundance, paving the way for lasting fulfillment and genuine happiness.

To practice bringing yourself back to a beautiful state of connection you must first be connected to yourself. The easiest and quickest way to do this is through your breath. A series of resources to support you to come home to a beautiful state is available at thesovereignwomansway.com.

CHAPTER 3

Universal Laws

Universal laws are the foundational principles that govern how the world works. There are literally thousands of laws; here, in *The Sovereign Woman's Way*, I will cover just a handful that are relevant to your journey. These laws possess their own consciousness and are consistent and unchanging in nature. By delving into the depths of these laws, you can harness their power to enhance the quality of your life and navigate your path with greater purpose and intention.

Many masters, artists, and scientists have channeled and learned how to work with the laws over the ages. For example, Nikola Tesla learned to work with the laws of magnetism and electricity. Tesla played a key role in the development and promotion of the alternating current (AC) electrical system, which was the foundation of modern electrical power distribution as well as the wireless transmission of electricity. He envisioned a world where electricity could be transmitted wirelessly over long distances. Another example, from a holistic healing perspective, is sound healing where practitioners work with the laws of tone, frequency, rhythm, and vibration.

To engage with the laws, it is imperative you first cultivate a belief in the existence and influence of them. This belief provides the necessary foundation for understanding the intricate workings of the laws and their impact on your life. By deepening your understanding of these laws, you can learn how to effectively collaborate with them, unlocking their potential to bring about positive change and transformation in your life.

The Law of Divine Oneness

Collective Consciousness awakens when we choose
to see the world through the eyes of Oneness.
—Anonymous

Let's talk about the first and the most fundamental law of the Universe, the Law of Divine Oneness. The Law of Divine Oneness states that all living beings are connected to one energy source, and this one energy source is connected to everything, and nothing exists outside of it. This includes your thoughts, feelings, emotions, and actions. They are directly connected to each other. And, therefore, whatever you think, feel, and do ripples out into this field of Divine Oneness.

When you know and live the embodiment of the Law of Divine Oneness, you realize that separation is just an illusion. That nothing or no one is separate from the other. Understanding this law is key to experiencing unconditional love, to freeing yourself from suffering states, and to coming back to a beautiful internal state of oneness.

Once you truly understand this principle, you will realize that the way you conduct yourself, the way you think, and the actions you take have a direct effect on this field and the world.

You will also understand that how you feel, act, and behave is impacted by the thoughts, feelings, actions, and beliefs of those around you and in your field of awareness. However, you can only ever control what you put out into this field of energy.

Within the field of Divine Oneness is the energy that created humanity. Therefore, you, like everyone, have a spark of Divine Oneness at the level of your soul. It is just your conditioning that keeps you captive and held in this Earthly plane, limiting what you believe is possible. But when you transcend these beliefs, and you understand that you are interconnected to everything and you are part of that Divine Oneness, anything is possible.

The Law of Divine Oneness transcends the Law of Polarity, which I will discuss soon. When you can see and heal the wounded parts of yourself, you transcend the light and the dark (polarity) through the healing integration of the divine masculine and feminine, and you access the wholeness and completeness within and connect to the oneness of all things.

The Law of Truth

According to Vianna Stibal's *Seven Planes of Existence*, the Law of Truth stands above all other laws, except for the Law of Compassion, which you must connect with to experience the unconditional love of the Creator of all that is. Many laws fall under the umbrella of the Law of Truth, including the Law of Cause and Effect, the Law of Free Agency, the Law of Wisdom, and the Law of Action, among others. The Law of Truth can be direct and straightforward. When connecting to the Law of Truth, do not expect any fluffiness or sugarcoating; it is about facing reality head-on. The Law of Truth is free from any opinions, perceptions, or judgment. It is just simply what is so, or what is!

The Law of Polarity

The Law of Polarity states that everything in the Universe has an opposite or opposing force and that these forces are dualistic in nature. For example:

- Light and Dark
- Left and Right
- Up and Down
- Inside and Outside

The Law of Polarity also suggests that these opposing forces are interconnected (as described in the Law of Divine Oneness), essentially one and the same just at opposing ends of the spectrum. For example, while a coin has two opposing sides, they, together, make the coin the single entity. It is the same with everything in your existence.

It is very important to understand this law, especially when looking at human behavior and when making changes in your life. In working with thousands of clients and doing inner healing and self reflection of my own, I can see how often people's behaviors and patterns mimic the Law of Polarity. Think of the pendulum effect discussed in Chapter 2: Human patterns of behavior swing back and forth. Recall the example of the relationship where one partner has a pattern of pleasing people. That overly accommodating person sacrifices their own needs to please another only to reach a threshold where it is no longer sustainable. Then they suddenly swing all the way to the opposite end of the spectrum where they withdraw all support and connection. These boundaries become so rigid that they feel isolated, alone, and often guilty, and eventually swing back into pleasing again. This pattern continues until they choose to stop.

Healing the wounds of love involves acknowledging both the negative and positive attributes that you display and realizing that every attribute, whether negative or positive, is within you as well as within others! This awareness can support you in interrupting the patterns and behaviors and is key to finding balance. It is important to know this law so that you can transcend its pull. The way to transcend its pull is to know the Laws of Balance and Harmony.

The Law of Balance

The Law of Balance suggests that there is a middle ground within the polarity of emotional states, behaviors, and programs. It suggests that at that middle ground, there is nonduality—equilibrium and harmony. The Law of Balance transcends the polarity of your life. I have found with many of my clients, and also with regards to myself and my behaviors, that there was always resistance to feeling and being in that center because outside of that center is where the highs and lows of life are. Many people need to feel those highs and lows and, thus, unknowingly create chaos and drama in their lives while avoiding the center.

I learned this during my awakening. When I experienced the highest of highs—the bliss, the rapture, being one with my beautiful Creator, feeling that energy coming through my body in its physical form—I wanted to reach those highs all the time. I wanted to stay in that high vibration. But eventually I would come crashing down and experience the exact opposite. For every high there is a low.

And the depths of the lows in your life equal the reach of the highs. When working with the Law of Balance, it's important to understand where you're at in any given moment and learn how to use the tools to heal through the sadness, heal through the lower vibrational patterns, so that you can bring yourself back into harmony, back into equilibrium, back into balance. The highs and lows are not meant to be for permanent residence; they exist to provide contrast, to help you identify and heal the pain, to experience joy and happiness so that you can peacefully reside in balance.

When I experienced my dark night of the soul, I cried out to the Creator. I cried out to God, "Why? Why do I have to feel the depths of this sadness?" To which the Creator reached out and said to me, "Because I want you to know what it's like to experience the full spectrum of what it is to be a human being." Remember, your soul came here to experience life. It came here to experience existence on this planet, to grow, and to evolve. And without having these experiences to learn from, you would only exist.

How can you work with the Law of Balance to come into more alignment? You work with the Law of Balance by understanding your position in that polarity. Where are you on the spectrum? What is needed and required to bring yourself back into balance, back into harmony?

You do that by coming home to yourself through daily practices that nourish and feed your body, mind, and soul.

Connect With the Creator

What do I mean by connect with the Creator? Remember the Creator can be God, the Universe, Spirit, Source, or whatever you choose to call the energy that created you. There are many ways to connect with the Creator. For some, it is through their connection to nature; for others, it is through meditation; and for others, it is in those moments of connection with their body, other beings, people, or animals.

Every individual has their own way of connecting with their Creator. Sometimes it can even be a combination of one or all of the above. One way that you can develop your own wisdom and trust with the Creator is to find your own answers to your questions without seeking validation or answers from outside influences; instead, obtain the answers from a deep connection with the highest truth, the energy that created you.

The Sovereign Woman's Way is here to help you connect more deeply to your inner wisdom, the truth of who you are, and to love yourself so that you can find the answers that lead to balance within so that you can live your purpose, the reason you came here. Only you can find these answers; no one else can tell you what they are. Don't get trapped swimming in a sea of information, searching outside of yourself for the answers. Anyone can get information; wisdom comes when you seek answers for yourself from within and they land for you in a way that raises your vibration.

Time spent connecting with the Creator, asking for wisdom, and asking questions that pertain to your day is how you start working with the Law of Balance.

The one question that I would ask every single day when I was in a space of not knowing, of being uncertain, was: "What do I need to know today, Creator? Guide me." I would get an oracle card, and I'd ask the Creator to guide the time we were spending together. When you trust and have absolute faith in your purpose, that you're here for a reason, that everything that's happening to you is happening for a divine purpose, even the card that you pull out of the deck has a meaning. It's up to you to find it, and the only way to do that is by being consciously aware and present.

Bring Awareness to the Polarities in Your Life
Polarity exists within you. Now is the time to reflect on personal traits or attributes. Do you believe that you are always kind? Where have you been unkind or mean? I guarantee you, it's there!

Awareness is the key that opens the door to your transformation. If you really want to be brave, take a look at a trait that you dislike in someone in your life and see where you also have this trait!

Move Stagnant Energy Through Your Body
When the emotions that you feel (or don't feel) are suppressed, they get stored in the body. This blocks your connection to your intuition and wisdom. By including the practice of KunYin® in my life, I have been able to quickly, often in less than an hour, move through emotions that previously had me stuck in a pattern for days.

IDENTIFY AND CLEAR LIMITING BELIEFS

Anytime a limiting belief is identified, I note it, clear it, and replace it with the perfect belief.

A replacement belief can be one that you would like to have rather than the existing limiting one you do have.

For example, in the previous chapter, I mentioned that I once believed:

- My body is shameful.
- I am afraid of intimacy.
- Pleasure is wrong.

These could be replaced with:

- My body is perfect, whole, and complete.
- I love my body.
- I accept my body.
- It is safe to be intimate.
- It is okay to feel pleasure.

Remember, each time you clear a limiting belief for yourself, you are healing on all four belief levels. So you are also healing your ancestors past and future, your past lives, your soul, and, essentially, as you are interconnected through the Law of Divine Oneness, you are healing and raising the collective consciousness of humanity. If that is not an incentive to do this work, I don't know what that is!

SELF REFLECTION THROUGH JOURNALING

Bringing awareness to the lessons that your body, mind, and soul are learning supports the creation of your new and empowering patterns and belief systems that will move you toward your best life. Each year, buy yourself a beautiful journal and document these lessons. One day, you will look back at all that you have learned and transformed within yourself and feel proud of the woman you have become.

If this is practiced consistently, you will quickly acquire the virtues needed to connect with the laws and to create more of what you desire in your life. Once you are able to work with the Law of Balance, you will find that your life is a magical existence.

The Law of Harmony

To work with the Law of Harmony, you must know and understand the Laws of Polarity and Balance. From the perspective of the individual, the Law of Harmony implies that there is a state of equilibrium within you. It's not about creating harmony outside of you but, rather, finding an inner state of harmony and then emanating that energy out into the world. Most people look outside of themselves to create what they want to see in the world. But the real access to changing the world, to having deeper connections with the people that you love and care about, is changing yourself. Understanding and knowing the Law of Harmony is critical if you want to create any authentic, positive, and lasting change in the world.

Recently, during a meditation, I was traveling through the planes in making my way up to the seventh plane to connect with the Creator of all that is. As I was ascending, I felt what I originally thought was the Law of Truth. But that was just my mind because the energy was very different from that of the Law of Truth. The Law of Truth can be very matter of fact. When working with it, there is no right or wrong, there is no duality, there is no polarity. There just is. And what I felt during that meditation was a very different kind of energy; it was a loving, kind, gentle, soft, feminine energy. I asked this energy, "Who are you?" In a beautiful, soft, and gentle tone, I received a message back: "I'm the Law of Harmony." I said, "Wow, how beautiful to be visited by you." And I asked the Law of Harmony, "Why have you visited me today?" To which she replied, "To know me, you must know yourself." And with that, she was gone. I left there pondering that answer. What did that mean? And I came to understand that in order to know the Law of Harmony, I must know harmony within myself, within my being. If I want to create harmony in the world, I must first learn how to create an inner sense of harmony, to remove the chaos, to detach from the drama, the negativity, the judgment of the world, and to find harmony within myself.

The Law of Compassion

The life you live today can be harsh—wars, separation in belief systems and values, the focus on survival, and the perpetual need to be validated and right in your point of view. It's easy to get caught up in it all and forget the simple things. In addition to the pressures of the external world, you are also forced to navigate the internal dialogue of self criticism that plagues your thoughts. The Law of Compassion teaches you to act toward yourself and others with patience, empathy, tolerance, understanding, and kindness—to accept yourself fully and completely without the need to be right, to demonstrate that someone else is wrong, or to prove anything. The Law of Compassion is the gateway to love. The most important aspect of compassion is to own your triggers and reactions to the world with a deep sense of compassion for yourself first and foremost. Likewise, true compassion involves withholding judgment and accepting people as they are, acknowledging that every person has their own unique experiences, points of view, and challenges and deserves respect and dignity. Without compassion, there is no access to love, the Creator, or Divine Oneness.

The Law of Cause and Effect

The Law of Cause and Effect is a consciousness to connect to and learn how to work with. When you connect to it, you will understand how you are a direct cause of the quality of your relationships and your life. The Law of Cause and Effect states the principle that whatever you do, think, or feel has a direct effect on the world around you. For example, if you plant an oak seed in good, fertile soil and nurture the seed with what it needs to grow—sun, water, and air—you will most likely end up with an oak tree. Consider that every interaction you have, every thought and action, is a seed being planted. Whatever you put out into the field of Divine Oneness, you will see the effect of.

To effectively work with the Law of Cause and Effect, you must have an acute awareness of your intent, thoughts, and actions. If you put out into the world positive thoughts and positive actions that come from love or pure intent, then that will ripple out into the world and, ultimately, through the Law of Karma, will come back to you at some point. It may not be in this lifetime; it may be in incoming lifetimes. The Law of Cause and Effect simply states that every action has a reaction. This law is how you expand your awareness to understand that you are the cause of your life, and this can bring you enormous power when you learn how to master your thoughts, actions, and behaviors. You cannot control anyone else's behaviors, but you can control your own!

The Law of Free Agency

The Law of Free Agency is a fundamental principle that affirms your inherent freedom and power to make choices and decisions based on your own will. It acknowledges that you have been granted the precious gift of free will as you embark on your Earthly journey to experience life in all its richness and complexity. Your choices, big and small, play a pivotal role in shaping the quality of your life and the nature of your relationships.

Embedded within the essence of free agency is the recognition that with great power comes great responsibility. It underscores the importance of making conscious choices that stem from pure intent and are aligned with serving not only your individual wellbeing but also the greater good. By approaching decision making with mindfulness and compassion, you can contribute positively to the tapestry of existence. As a human being, inevitably there will be times that you make poor decisions. You are not always going to make the best decisions, and often this can only be seen after the fact with the gift of hindsight. In these cases, it is important to remember to take stock of the lesson learned, have compassion for yourself, and take responsibility for the impact of your decisions and actions.

Choices that arise from lower vibrational states of suffering, such as revenge, greed, jealousy, hurt, or regret, can sow seeds of discord and disharmony in your life. The interconnectedness of all things, as reflected in the Laws of Cause and Effect and Divine Oneness, highlights how your actions and decisions reverberate through the fabric of existence. By cultivating awareness and making choices rooted in love, empathy, and integrity, you can navigate the complexities of life with grace and create a more harmonious reality for yourself and those around you.

To work with the laws that govern the Universe, you must cultivate the virtues that will be discussed in more detail in the next chapter. These virtues serve as the building blocks for creating a harmonious relationship with the universal laws, allowing you to align with the natural order of the workings of the world as you know it, including the cosmos!

CHAPTER 4

Vices and Virtues

Vices

Vices are negative or destructive behaviors that impact an individual, a relationship, or the community. The three main vices that impact the human experience of growth are:

- ♥ Self criticism
- ♥ Self sabotage
- ♥ Self doubt

SELF CRITICISM

Self criticism is the silent, pervasive voice that tells you that you are not good enough.

The desire to prove your worth and be loved is so strong, it filters into all aspects of your life and relationships. Once, I opened up to a dear friend about how disappointed I was with myself after an event that we ran, and she told me that the way I was speaking to myself was a form of self abuse. I would never have even noticed it had she not mentioned it because it was shrouded in high standards and it had served me well. I would tell myself that I had high standards as a way of berating myself to do better, to achieve more. I told myself it was just who I was! All your beliefs do serve you in some way. This drove me to constantly strive to improve, to create world-class events and training programs, but at what cost? It cost me fulfillment, being satisfied and content, happy and productive.

Self criticism can look like high standards, comparing yourself to others, perfectionism, or taking unnecessary fault or blame. It's that little voice in your head that tells you:

- I shouldn't have done that.
- It's all my fault.
- I'm to blame.
- I could have done better.
- I am so stupid.
- No one is going to love me.
- No one will want what I have to offer.
- I am ugly.
- I am fat.
- I look tired and old.

Can you relate to any of these thoughts? Sometimes that little voice inside your head is not even yours! Maybe it is the echo of a parent, sibling, relative, or childhood friend. If you grew up in an environment where you were constantly criticized or held to high standards, you may have internalized these messages and developed a habit of self criticism. Until I realized the impact it was having on me, I happily repeated something my mother used to say to me: "If something is worth doing, it's worth doing properly!" I would procrastinate on everything because if there wasn't time for doing it "properly," I wouldn't do it at all! I have since replaced this with a belief I heard at a seminar I attended: "If something is worth doing, it's worth doing poorly!" This has changed my life! Now I give things a go even if I can't do it properly the first time.

I will keep improving each time, getting wiser, smarter, faster, and more confident. Eventually, if I keep going long enough without giving up, I become masterful in what I set my intentions to.

Past experiences of trauma, abuse, or bullying can also contribute to the development of self criticism. If you have been through traumatic experiences, you may internalize negative messages about yourself and develop a habit of self criticism as a coping mechanism, as a way to make sense of why the abuse happened. Once you become aware of that little voice in your head, you have the power to change it!

- ♥ What does the little critical voice inside your head tell you?
- ♥ Is it even your voice or does it belong to someone else?
- ♥ How has it served you?
- ♥ What has it cost you?

SELF SABOTAGE

Self sabotage is a pattern of behavior where you undermine your own success, happiness, and wellbeing. It is linked to self criticism and a lack of self worth, and it can manifest as procrastination, perfectionism, substance abuse, or avoiding opportunities that can lead to success. Fears, such as fear of failure, fear of intimacy, fear of success, or fear of rejection, can lead to sabotaging behaviors.

In many cases, the fears lie hidden in beliefs in the subconscious, beliefs formed in your younger years. Once brought to the conscious, identifying and releasing them can prevent self sabotaging behaviors. In Chapter 6, I will discuss self discipline because, once identified, self discipline as a practice is a great way to overcome patterns of sabotage.

- ♥ Where in your life do you self sabotage?
- ♥ What has it cost you?
- ♥ What could be the underlying reasons for self sabotage?

Self Doubt

Self doubt, a common emotional state characterized by a lack of confidence or belief in oneself, can have an impact on your mindset and behavior. It often manifests through overthinking, incessant questioning of decisions, and the tendency to replay situations repeatedly in your mind.

The fear of rejection and aversion to taking risks can create a barrier to personal growth and self discovery. If you succumb to self doubt, you may find yourself leading a life marked by caution, staying safe, and reluctance to step outside your comfort zone. This avoidance of risks limits opportunities for exploration and learning.

True confidence is often found in moments of uncertainty and challenge, where you must venture beyond your comfort zone and on to the metaphorical "skinny branches" of life. It is through these experiences that you can cultivate resilience, discover hidden strengths, and nurture a deeper sense of self assurance. By embracing these challenges and pushing past the boundaries of comfort, you can unlock your full potential and embark on a journey of self discovery and growth.

Self doubt is the number-one killer of dreams, so you must get out of your comfort zone to overcome this vice. With the right support and mindset, it is possible to navigate through its challenges and emerge stronger and more confident on the other side and know what you are truly made of!

Virtues

Because there is a natural duality to all of existence, there is an opposing energy to vices, and it is called virtues. What exactly are virtues?

Virtues are positive qualities and attributes that you acquire over lifetimes. As you grow and evolve, you deepen your ability to master these qualities. Your soul yearns to learn virtues, as this is partly why you incarnate on Earth. Throughout your life's journey, you need to acquire and master virtues so that you can grow and evolve and fulfill your soul's purpose.

You learn virtues all the time; however, you may not have any conscious awareness of it because you are often not present in your life and are just running from one conditioned program to another. It is important to know when you are learning virtues so that you can declare that lesson or learning experience as completed. Without your conscious awareness and declaration of the lesson being completed, you may find yourself continuing to learn the same lessons over and over again! Some virtues can be easier to learn than others, which can take lifetimes to master.

There is a difference between knowing a virtue, understanding it with your mind, and being the physical embodiment of that particular virtue. Knowing it with your mind or practicing it occasionally will not cut it! You need to master it. True mastery is about consistently personifying the virtues, especially when the going gets tough.

It's easy to say you have faith in God, but when you're tested, how much faith do you really have? It's easy to say that you believe that everything is happening in divine timing, but how much belief do you really have when the lesson is painful to learn? How much trust and patience do you really have when you want something *now*?

For example, you may know what kindness is. However, when it comes to actively practicing kindness, little acts of kindness go a long way. Smiling at a stranger, giving way at an intersection, being calm and kind to another parent when a child is having a meltdown in the supermarket, giving a compliment to a stranger. In my experience, these little things can be overlooked when you are in the throes of life. The most difficult act of kindness that I have experienced is kindness toward myself—being kind to my body, having a schedule that allows time for rest, quieting my overactive and critical mind. These little acts of self kindness go a long way toward improving my experience of life.

When things go differently than you expect, do you allow that critical voice to take over or is the voice inside you kind and gentle? It took awareness and practice for me to cultivate a kind internal dialogue with myself. I realized this was a virtue I was relatively new at experiencing. There is also a difference between acquiring a virtue and deepening it. The ego will say, "I have acquired that virtue," but the higher self knows that you are always on a journey of growth, so mastery is the goal. Acquiring and mastering virtues is a very important part of the evolution of your soul, impacting your experience of love, joy, and what it is to live a beautiful life that is connected and filled with love.

There are hundreds of virtues; however, the ones that I have selected here specifically relate to my own personal journey, to deepening the sense of love and connection that I have with myself. I used to think that love was somewhere outside of me, but now I know it is a way of being that I need to cultivate inside myself.

BEAUTY

Beauty really is in the eye of the beholder and can be many things, people, places, and experiences. This can include the beauty of nature, the beauty of art, the beauty of the synchronicities of life, the beauty in another's body, or the beauty in your own body. Beauty can inspire creativity and bring a sense of joy, appreciation, and wonder into your life.

The virtue of beauty is about training yourself to see the beauty in each and every moment and aspect of life. Mastering the virtue of beauty is training yourself to pause, focus, and be present in the current moment. Beauty is witnessed and experienced in the present. To acquire the virtue of beauty, you must also develop the virtues of presence and focus. How do you cultivate a deep respect and wonder for the magnificence of the world around you? You bring your awareness into the present and focus on what is beautiful about this moment, person, or experience. When you are present enough and focus on what is good and beautiful, you will see and experience beauty all around you.

Through a sixty-minute class in the practice of KunYin®, the instructors take women through a journey of experiencing the beauty, strength, and power of their emotional and physical bodies. It is a great tool to cultivate this practice and strengthen the muscle in the virtue of beauty. To experience the beauty of your body, you can try a class for free by going to the KunYin® website, kunyin.com.au.

BRAVERY

Bravery inspires you to act in spite of your fears and in spite of the challenges you face. The virtue of bravery encourages you to move forward with strength and determination. The virtues of focus, clarity, and commitment work hand in hand with bravery; there must be something at stake for you to be brave. What you desire must be greater than the fears that hold you captive. You must be clear and focused on the brave actions that you take.

To be called to bravery, there must be a strong purpose pulling you forward. It must be something that you desire—love can do this! Being brave will leave you feeling empowered in knowing that you have the ability to face and overcome your fears. For those that witness acts of bravery, it can leave them feeling inspired to also take action in their own life.

To live a life according to your own rules, to live to the beat of your own drum, you are going to have to live in your truth, in the authenticity of who you really are. And, very often, going after those things that you desire, breaking the genetic beliefs and programs that you've inherited, takes bravery. In doing so, you live life as a sovereign being.

CLARITY

The virtue of clarity embodies being understood and clear. It is essential in communication, decision making, problem solving, and in your ability to trust and be trusted. It is especially important in relationships and manifesting your desires. Fear, doubt, and limiting beliefs will impact your ability to truly embrace the virtue of clarity. You must work on identifying and clearing your fears if you want to truly master this virtue. If not, all that you envision or see for yourself will be filtered through these fears. When fears are cleared, you will be able to know and embody clarity in your life—from what you desire to what you want to create. The fewer distractions, obstructions, and conflicts you have in your life, the more you will become open for obtaining clarity. Clearing fears combined with the virtue of clarity can support you while working with the Law of Truth, and the Law of Truth can support you in achieving your life's purpose. So the more clarity you have, the more effectively you will communicate and the faster you will make decisions and take action. The faster you are able to take action, the happier you will be, the more content you will feel in your choices, and the more fulfilled you will be in love and in your life.

CLEANLINESS

Cleanliness means being free from impurities and demonstrating respect for your body, mind, and living environment. In the face of life's challenges, it can be tempting to overlook these simple yet essential practices that contribute to your wellbeing.

There have been instances in my own life when the weight of difficulties made it a struggle to even get out of bed, let alone engage in basic self care routines like brushing my teeth. However, I have found that transforming seemingly mundane activities, such as taking a shower, into acts of reverence and self honoring can have a profound impact on my overall wellbeing.

By approaching personal hygiene rituals with intention and utilizing chemical-free products, I am able to engage in a mindful process of cleaning and rejuvenating my body. Similarly, maintaining a clean and clutter-free living space through regular tidying and decluttering not only creates a harmonious environment but also fosters a deep sense of self respect.

Returning to a state of cleanliness and embracing practices that promote self discipline, like cultivating healthy habits of tidiness and organization, can serve as a form of self care and nurturing. Ultimately, this dedication to self love through cleanliness can lead to a profound sense of self worth and wellbeing.

COMMITMENT

The virtue of commitment is about dedication to a goal, objective, or purpose. It means staying true to the promises that you've made to yourself and others despite the challenges that you may face or the obstacles that may come your way. If you are able to have and keep anything of value, a certain level of mastery in the virtue of commitment is required.

Those that consistently demonstrate the virtue of commitment are people who others come to trust. This is especially important when building lasting relationships—whether romantic, platonic, or professional.

Through the practice of mastery in this virtue, you can expand and grow, which is exactly what your soul wants to do. It takes perseverance to stay committed to a path, purpose, relationship, or course of action—especially when the going gets tough. By developing and strengthening your virtue of commitment, you can push yourself to places you've never been before, going over and above, in and outside of your comfort zone; learn new skills and new abilities; and become somebody with resilience.

Commitment—following through on what you desire—is critical when it comes to living a life that you love and experiencing self love. It's breaking old patterns, beliefs, and programming and being persistent. It's showing up every day, as you said you would, and honoring your word. It is following through; it is knowing what you want, moving toward it, and taking the actions to get there.

COMPASSION

Compassion is your ability to have a sense of empathy for the suffering of others and especially for yourself. Compassion is critical when it comes to love, to relationships, to living your soul's purpose. Compassion deepens as you let go of suffering states, judgment, and criticism and grow in mastering the virtues over a lifetime.

CONTENTMENT

Contentment may seem like a very ordinary, boring, or simple virtue; however, it is absolutely necessary for living a fulfilling life. You can strive and achieve the greatest heights in success and never experience contentment. A lack of contentment can lead you to getting exactly what you want but without any fulfillment. For those of you driven toward growth, the desire for new levels of attainment will always be present. Accepting these desires as well as your present situation can support you in being content no matter where you are in life and no matter the results you have obtained or are yet to obtain. It's imperative to understand and know the virtue of contentment so that you can be satisfied with everything that you have and that you are in any given moment to experience peace within that place.

DETACHMENT

The virtue of detachment is the state of being committed to something or someone wholeheartedly without being attached to the outcome. It is different from dissociation, where one cuts off the feelings associated with an outcome or person. Detachment is not disconnection; it is not cutting people out of your life. It is approaching the situation or person to which you are attached with an open heart, committed to the desired outcome but unattached to it. To be detached, you must realize and practice knowing that you are whole and complete without anything or anyone else.

You may practice detachment in your relationships by no longer seeking approval. Any forms of codependency or dependency will have to die for you to practice detachment. Healing your fears and past wounds around betrayal, abandonment, denial, separation, and judgment will support you in detaching from the outcome with an open heart. This doesn't mean you give up on your dreams and desires; it just means you are no longer controlled by them.

When you master the virtue of detachment, you understand and embody self belief, independence, and a knowing that you can live and flourish without the need to be dependent on people, places, or things.

You might often become attached to material things, like homes, money, jewelry, or any other possessions. Many of these attachments imprison you to the unconscious beliefs and conditioning that created them. For example, many people, my past self included, are so attached to the dream of owning a property, having investments, having fancy jewelry and cars that they become a prisoner to the life they have just to keep them, fearful that they might lose them if they stopped working so hard and enjoyed more of life. Don't get me wrong, I still have those things, and I enjoy them; however, I am not attached to them. When I decided that my freedom and my sovereignty were more important than possessions, I was able to prioritize what is really important and live in alignment without the fear that I might lose them.

DEVOTION

Devotion differs from commitment because devotion requires love, respect, wisdom, and consistency as well as commitment. Devotion is a deep feeling to a person or a cause centered in love, loyalty, and reverence. Devotion can also be in the context of religion or spirituality.

But in the context of this book and your soul's evolution, I invite you to take it a little bit further, out of the constructs of group consciousness and into the devotion to yourself. Being devoted to the love you have for yourself is not just a fleeting feeling. It's not just something that you do every now and then. It is a pattern of behavior that you cultivate consistently with love and respect on a daily basis.

When you acquire the virtue of devotion, it draws you into a deep sense of peace. It's very different from the energy of passion or desire, which can be impacted by the polarity of uncertainty and fears and create the highs and lows of physical attraction. Devotion is a state of being that comes with a full-bodied sense of knowing and certainty.

DIGNITY

To embody the virtue of dignity, you must be in the state of knowing and being worthy of honor and respect. Dignity is having respect for yourself, your emotions, your body, and your boundaries. Speaking your truth from love and honoring your word to yourself and others are ways that you can cultivate the virtue of dignity.

Behaviors such as belittling yourself, disrespecting your body and your boundaries, self criticism, and ignoring your own emotions can be undignified. Your inner world reflects your outer world. So, if you are being undignified to yourself, how is that showing up in how you treat others?

FAITH

In the pursuit of what you desire, truly fulfilling your life's purpose, and experiencing a deeper sense of love, you are going to have to have faith because the ways that the Creator wants you to learn your lessons and to evolve are not the ways that your human brain thinks that they should be. People often have ideas about how life should be, about how relationships should be, and essentially they "should should should" all over themselves. And when something doesn't turn out the way that they think it "should," they lose faith in the process, and they lose hope. The virtue that you need to acquire above all else is faith—faith that no matter what is happening in your life, there is a greater plan, there is a greater reason and purpose for the things that are happening. Faith is knowing that life is happening for you, not to you. And that takes an extraordinary leap of trust to live with and can take a lifetime to master.

It also is important to declare the lessons along the way so that your faith doesn't continue to be tested. It's important to acknowledge a lesson as you learn it and as you acquire the virtue. You can say, "That didn't turn out the way I expected, but I can see the bigger picture. I have a higher perspective." Declare it complete and move forward in faith knowing that everything is exactly the way it is meant to be.

FOCUS

Focus. Why is focus as a virtue important to acquire? Well, look at the Law of Attraction and look at the Law of Cause and Effect; they state that what you focus on you will attract. It is, therefore, very important to be the master of your mind and understand what it is that you are focusing on. Are you focusing on the best possible outcome for yourself in every situation? Or are you focusing on what might go wrong? Are you focusing on what you want? Or are you focusing on what you don't want? Many women I talk to during healing sessions consistently tell me what they don't desire, what they don't want, what's not working. And with that mindset, they're attracting more of those very things into their lives. You attract what you are a vibration for. You attract the energy that you are an energetic match with. So through consistent focusing on what you desire and what you want, you will attract more of it into your life.

FORGIVENESS
Forgiveness is a big one.

It is important to master the virtue of forgiveness because holding on to anger, upset, resentment, hurt, and grudges is harmful for your relationships, for your nervous system, your body, and for your emotional state. Holding on to these emotions can create dis-ease in your body because, remember, emotions are energy in motion, and emotions that don't move through your body get stuck in your cells and organs. Resentments can be held in your liver and your kidneys and can create problems with alcoholism and other addictions. You may hold on to these emotions because you're not sure how to process them or how to forgive. You may think that forgiveness is for the other person, but, when you forgive, truly forgive, it is a gift that you give yourself. It is the freedom that you give yourself to experience more of those beautiful emotions like love and happiness and joy. And even if you're not quite at the stage of forgiveness, at a minimum, work toward feeling acknowledgment and acceptance of the situation for now.

Sometimes when I'm working with my clients, they're not quite ready to forgive. In my experience, I never push anyone to forgive because it's not going to be real until such time as they're ready, which, often, is only once they experience the impact of not forgiving, when they can see the harm that it's creating in their lives and other relationships. Forgiving doesn't mean that you are condoning somebody else's behavior; it doesn't mean that you are saying it's okay. It means that you forgive because you choose to detach with love from that person's behavior, to not allow that behavior to have power over your life anymore. It is the greatest act of self love. It's freeing yourself up from all of the internal tension, conflict, and potential dis-ease in your body by letting go of those lower vibrational emotions.

GRATITUDE

Gratitude is the highest vibration next to love. When you are grateful, you cannot be ungrateful at the same time. It comes down to a matter of focus. By choosing gratitude, you raise your vibration and call in more of what you are grateful for. Practicing the virtue of gratitude on a daily basis can be life-changing. By finding the things in your life that you can be grateful for, especially if you are in a dark night of the soul, you will lift yourself up out of the darkness. When it feels impossible to find something to be grateful for, just be grateful for your breath. Sometimes you can even be grateful for waking up in the morning. It's a matter of perspective and focus. And when you cultivate an art, a practice, or an attitude of gratitude, as they like to say, you can really transform how you feel about yourself and raise your vibration. I often recommend the daily practice of saying out loud, "I'm so happy and grateful," and then writing it down to reinforce it. You can gradually increase this practice to include adding what you are grateful for. Notice the change that it makes in your life; notice how much more of what you desire comes into your life.

INNOCENCE

I believe that each person comes into this world innocent. Despite being raised in a Catholic family, I have chosen to disconnect from the consciousness of belief in original sin, which is the concept that because of Adam and Eve's sin, all human beings are born with a sinful nature and are separated from God. I believe that, at the soul level, humans are all innocent; that it is only through life experiences, including that of past lives, that humans feel shame, blame, guilt, regret, and many other lower vibration emotional states. The virtue of innocence takes you back to the purity of your soul before you succumbed to conditioning and limiting beliefs over your lifetime. There is nothing you need to do to purify yourself; the only requirement is for you to feel if this resonates with you, and if so, choose to believe in your innocence. You are, after all, what you believe yourself to be!

INTEGRITY

Integrity should not be confused with morality; integrity is not right or wrong. Integrity is deeply personal, and no one can tell you what is or what is not integrity for you. Only you can do that by feeling what aligns with your truth and values. Integrity works hand in hand with the virtue of wisdom.

To me, integrity is defined as:

- Being aligned with my own values.
- Doing what I said I would do.
- Doing what I know to do.
- Doing what I know to do even if I didn't say that I would do it.
- Honoring my word.
- Honoring myself.
- Being on time.
- Restoring my word when I know that I cannot follow through on it.
- Keeping an empowering perspective on my life.

If you feel that you lack integrity in your life, go on an integrity treasure hunt! A little self reflection exercise that I like is to look at all the areas of my life where:

- I have given my word to someone and not followed through.
- I have given my word to myself and not followed through.
- I have had a conversation to restore that word, which means recommitting or acknowledging that I have not completed or done what I said I would do.
- I want to restore my integrity around my finances, so I pay all my bills on time or recommit to payment plans.

Living outside of this integrity can cause you to lose trust in yourself and your power in your life. I remember being at one of my workplaces, and I had a friend that I would meet for morning tea most days. I remember calling her to meet me one morning. I told her that I would be there in five minutes. She laughed at me. I asked her why she was laughing, and she said, "Yeah, right!" meaning that I would not be on time. I reflected on this a little later in the day and noticed how anytime I said I would do something, even if it was important or meant a lot to me, she would not take me seriously. I certainly was not someone who didn't want to be taken for my word. So, from that day on, I made a conscious effort to follow through on my word and to honor my commitments no matter how big or small they seemed. This has given me an enormous sense of pride and honor in who I am as well as workability in my life.

KINDNESS

Kindness is humble yet impactful. A small act of kindness to a stranger can transform their life, and an act of kindness toward yourself can transform your life. Practicing kindness toward yourself is not always easy, especially when self criticism kicks in, when the fears, the doubts, the worries, and the business of life creeps in. It's important to replace that critical voice with the voice of kindness. How would that feel for you? How could you transform your life simply by practicing kindness toward yourself and, in return, kindness toward others?

PATIENCE

Patience is having faith and trust that things are happening exactly as they are meant to be happening in divine timing. Faith, trust, and patience all go hand in hand. A lack of faith, trust, and patience can lead to your life being driven by fears and a need to control situations. This control manifests as impatience and frustration. So the next time things don't happen as fast as you'd like them to, or the next time you're stuck in traffic, take a deep breath and trust that it's all exactly as it's meant to be.

PRESENCE

Cultivating the virtue of presence requires consistent awareness. Presence is an important virtue to master because if you don't master it, you will find yourself living either in the past or in the future. If you are focused on the past, you may experience feelings of regret, sadness, or loss. If you are experiencing future-based thinking, you may feel anxiety, irritation, or nervousness. Moreover, the future hasn't arrived, and it may not arrive.

In 2022, I decided that my only goal for 2023 was to practice being present in every moment. Why did I choose that as my only goal? Because I had been fretting over a future that didn't exist, a future that I wanted so badly to create, but it wasn't happening in my time. And I found that I was missing out on valuable, beautiful experiences with people that I loved because I couldn't be present with them. In 2023, I chose to be present in each moment, and I was able to experience so much joy, so much beauty, and so much happiness for my life because I wasn't missing anything. I wasn't missing the beauty of a hummingbird; the beauty of an eagle flying above; or the beauty of an experience with somebody that I love. I was fully present at that moment. Cultivating and mastering the virtue of presence is one of the greatest gifts that you will give yourself. It is very powerful.

PURE INTENT

Pure intent is a lesser-known virtue, and it takes conscious awareness and a knowing of yourself to cultivate. Pure intent is the ability to go inward and ask yourself, "Are the things that I desire in integrity for me? Are my desires coming from a place of pure intent, for the highest and best for all of humanity, including myself? Is it just to benefit me? Or is it to benefit somebody else at my own expense?"

Sometimes you may desire something and use shame, manipulation, guilt, or domination as a way to obtain it. These patterns can be quite subtle and easily missed, especially if you are mimicking behaviors displayed to you in your developmental years. You may have been raised in a family where you were guilted or manipulated into doing things that you didn't want to.

Maybe you've said the following:

- ♡ Mummy will be sad if you don't do xyz . . .
- ♡ Look, now you made Daddy angry, be a good girl.
- ♡ You deserve to be punished.
- ♡ You should be ashamed of yourself.

In many cases, you don't even have to say words to be manipulative; it can simply be an action, like stonewalling, shutting down, or a look to get what you want. These are all mechanisms to control and manipulate the will of others and are not pure intent.

If behaviors are driven by less than pure intent, then the results will be a less than ideal outcome, especially due to the Law of Cause and Effect. What you put out there you will get back. Bringing awareness by understanding yourself and your patterns can support you to understand what the intentions behind your actions are and support you in moving forward with pure intent. It is critical for achieving the best outcomes in your life.

SURRENDER

I bet you're asking, "Why do I need to surrender?" Because life is not always going to go the way you plan. Life doesn't show up the way that you think it should.

Surrender is a deliberate choice to stop resisting what is. It can involve accepting a situation, letting go of control, or yielding to divine timing. Surrender often entails letting go of personal desires or agendas in favor of the higher purpose for your life. In surrender, you are still open to the possibilities in the flow of divine timing but without the need to control them.

Surrender is not giving up nor is it defeat. Defeat is the belief that you have failed or have been overcome by the situation. Giving up can suggest that you abandon your efforts and end up being disengaged and disappointed. Your mother doesn't show up the way you think she should or your partner doesn't show up the way you think they should. The more you try and push up against this truth, the more resistance you will experience. There comes a time where you must practice discernment on when to surrender and how to surrender without feeling like you're giving up or being defeated.

I used to believe that in order to surrender, I needed to be in physical pain. I needed to have reached a threshold where I couldn't possibly go any further. I finally learned that maybe I could surrender before I reached that point. What if any time I experienced resistance, I could let go and surrender to the bigger picture, surrender to the Creator's plan? What if I didn't have to make things happen? How would this release me from pain?

TRUST
The three elements of the virtue of trust to master are:

- ♡ Trust in yourself, also known as self trust.
- ♡ Trust in your Creator.
- ♡ Trust in your body.

Self trust is the belief and confidence in your own abilities, judgment, and decisions. It involves having faith in your own capabilities, values, and instincts. Self trust comes from overcoming times of uncertainty and difficulty and being kind to yourself as you learn life's lessons. When you trust yourself, you believe that you can handle challenges, make good decisions, and feel comfortable with who you are.

Self trust is an essential component of trust in general. Trust should not be instantly given over to another; that would be foolish. The more you trust yourself, the more discernment you will have regarding who to trust in life.

Trust in your Creator, trust that you are a divine spark of creation, is a level of trust in love. It is trusting that you are already loved just as you are, and you will be taken care of. Any limiting beliefs, grudges, resentments, or anger toward the Creator can limit your relationship with the source of your creation and, ultimately, yourself.

Trust in your body is so important. I believe that you chose the body that you incarnated into for this lifetime. You chose this body so that you and it could experience life together. If this concept is foreign to you, take a moment to think about why you may have chosen this body. What has it taught you?

I am five-foot-nothing, and when people meet me in person, they are often surprised at how tiny I am. When they see me on the screen or online, they think I'm much bigger than I actually am. This is because I have never really seen myself as tiny or small. I believe I chose a small stature so that I could grow my voice and have people feel my presence through my energy rather than my physicality.

So many women that I work with have the belief that their body has let them down. That in some way their body is to blame for illness, not being beautiful enough, not skinny enough, not looking a particular way, or for them not achieving something they wanted to do. Your body is always working for you, and your cells feel it when you say negative things about them and react accordingly.

Fears, past hurts, and betrayals all get in the way of truly learning to embody and master the virtue of trust. But when the three elements of trust are embodied, you begin to truly experience it. In many cases, you lose the need to place too much emphasis on trust in others because you trust yourself and your Creator, and that is all you need!

WISDOM

Wisdom is not only the ability to make sound decisions and choices, it is about practicing discernment in all areas of life based on introspection, empathy, and insight.

Wisdom comes with experience through awareness, presence, observation, and contemplation. It is a combination of all the other virtues that support you in your growth and evolution. It's important to create space in your day to pause and understand what is happening around you and within you so that you can receive wisdom from the Creator.

Create a daily practice to connect to the Creator, and meditate and ask for guidance and wisdom in your life. Learn from your mistakes; learn from the things that didn't go the way you thought they should. Take the lessons and understand from them what virtue you were acquiring so that you can gain the wisdom that you need to take your life to the next level.

## CHAPTER 5

Love—What Is It Anyway?

How do you understand what love is?

Your beliefs about love are shaped in the very early stages of your life, predominantly by how you need to behave to be loved by your parents in order to receive their nurturing, safety, and protection.

A lack of love or nurturing can create a distorted perception of what love truly is, and experiences of pain, hurt, and suffering in childhood can significantly influence and mold your beliefs about love. Even if you receive an abundance of love during your early stages, life's experiences can create alternative core beliefs about what love is. Many of these beliefs are not what love really is.

For instance, I once had a client who, as a young boy, found that his mother was unable to provide him with the love he craved. She was busy with other children, running the household, and taking care of her extended family. It wasn't until he had an accident while playing and injured himself and his mother came rushing to his aid that he felt loved. In the preadolescent years, children are constantly learning strategies to be loved, acknowledged, rewarded, and nurtured. When a strategy works, it goes into their subconscious and is called upon time and time again when there is a need for love. For my client, his mother's behavior linked receiving love with experiencing physical pain. He developed the belief that he needed to be in pain to be deserving of love.

This belief led him to unconsciously seek out situations filled with pain, followed by drama and chaos. Unfortunately, this pattern took a toll on his health and his intimate relationships. It created a strain on his relationship with his wife, who was constantly having to support him and be strong for him through his pain. She put her own needs aside for decades, which allowed hurt and resentment set in. It was difficult, although not impossible, to unwind the old patterns and create new ones. But this story ends well; both of these people were able to communicate with each other and identify the patterns and how each of them had contributed to the state of the relationship. They were able to see their conditioned beliefs and how they played out and, ultimately, changed them.

Another client was sexually abused by her father. Since a father's role in life is to love and protect his child, she formed the subconscious belief that if her father is supposed to love her and yet abuses her, then love is abuse. This distorted view of love caused her to attract a plethora of men into her life that also abused her. As she had developed little self worth and did not have a role model to show her what love really was, she went well into her thirties before she healed and cleared this belief.

It's not uncommon to subconsciously create self destructive behaviors or patterns in your quest for love and care that may push love further away. It is essential for you to be aware of these deeply ingrained beliefs that no longer serve you.

To understand more about beliefs that you have created about love, think about the following:

- Whose love did you crave the most while growing up? Your mother or your father's love? You may have wanted both, but which one did you *crave* the *most*?
- Who did you have to be to receive this love?

For example, when I was a little girl, I craved my father's love the most, largely because it was the least frequently given. He worked a lot, and if he was not working, he was in the garden or out playing cards with his friends in the local espresso bars. To earn my father's love, I had to be a good girl, do what I was told, and make him proud. This showed up in my life as always trying to impress my father with my achievements and good behavior.

Beliefs I created were:

- I have to be a good girl to be loved by my father.
- I have to be good to get my father's attention.
- I have to do what I am told to be loved.
- Men will only love me if I am good.
- Love is conditional.

As you identify and let go of all limiting beliefs that you have created about love, you can replace them with the highest truth of love. The highest truth of love is that you are love and you are created from love. Many people believe that true love is unconditional, but I call bullshit on that. All love is conditional. You are human, and if you respect yourself and your boundaries, you will have conditions on how you will and will not be treated. The only love that is unconditional comes from the Creator. As you work toward fostering healthier boundaries, a deeper respect for yourself, and knowing your worth and your perceptions of love, you will align more closely with how you genuinely want to experience and understand love.

To get a full list of limiting beliefs on love, turn to Chapter 11's "Love Beliefs" list and see if any of them resonate with you. Alternatively, download the free list at thesovereignwomansway.com.

What Is Love?

Love is the only thing that is real; everything else is an illusion.

So what is love? To answer this question, travel back to Ancient Greece and Ancient Greek mythology. According to Greek mythology, there are five different types of love:

1. Eros
2. Philia
3. Storge
4. Agape
5. Philautia

Eros is associated with deep, passionate, fiery love, sensuality, romance, and desire. In Greek mythology, Eros was the god of love and desire and was known for shooting arrows at people to inspire romantic love in them. Eros represents the often intense emotional and physical attraction that can exist between two individuals, the feeling of your heart racing, the excitement that you have when you think about the other person, the feeling of hummingbirds in your chest. Through the experience of Eros, you begin to understand the pleasure-filled experience of living in a human body and exploring that intimately with another.

The next type of love is Philia, pronounced FIL-ee-uh. Philia is a deep sense of trust and loyalty amongst friends, like a sisterhood, and it goes beyond affection or attraction. Philia is where common experiences, values, and interests are shared, where the love is reciprocated in equal measure, and where both parties mutually benefit from the connection within the relationship. It emphasizes the importance of genuine friendship, loyalty, trust, and mutual respect.

Storge, pronounced STOR-jay, was known by the ancient Greeks to represent a familial love, the kind of love that develops between family members—the love of parents, of siblings, cousins, and other relatives. Storge provides the foundation for strong family units, ensuring that you feel nurtured and cared for.

Agape, pronounced as ah-GAH-peh, is unconditional, selfless love. Agape includes a love for God, a love for your Creator. I also believe that agape love is essential for cultivating the kind of love that you desire in your physical life, understanding and having that connection to a source greater than yourself. Agape encompasses love for all humanity and encourages people to contribute positively to society by considering the needs of others.

The fifth type of love is lesser known and discussed. Philautia, pronounced FIL-aw-tee-uh, is the idea of loving yourself; it was explored by Ancient Greek philosophers like Aristotle and Plato. They believed that self love is a prerequisite for loving others, as it serves as the foundation for the virtue of love in all relationships. This is the foundational principle upon which this book has been written. You have been programmed and conditioned to seek Storge, Eros, Philia, and Agape, but what gets overlooked so often is the love of self. I truly believe that all other types of love lack authenticity if the love of self is not present. First you must learn to give this love to yourself, and only then can you receive it authentically from others. Philautia complements you, it does not seek to fill a void within you.

You are only able to love others to the extent that you love yourself. You are only able to have compassion for others to the extent you can have compassion for yourself. Everything begins and ends with you. This is what it is to love. Love is not an act. There are acts of love, absolutely, but love is not an action. I believe that love is a state of being. It's a state of being when you are passionate in desire, pleasure, or sensuality while experiencing the energy of Eros; it is being loving, connected, and nurturing with your family members or your children while experiencing the love of Storge. When you feel the trust and loyalty within sisterhood, Philia is present. And if you feel that beautiful love and protection that comes from your connection with God, then you are experiencing the energy of Agape.

In modern psychology and self help literature, the concept of self love continues to be explored and emphasized as an important component of mental health, self esteem, and overall wellbeing. Cultivating a healthy sense of self love is seen as essential for personal growth, resilience, and fulfilling relationships with others. Therefore, Philautia, the love for oneself, continues to be a relevant and valuable concept in contemporary discussions about self care, self compassion, and personal development. It's important to understand these various aspects of love because if there is love missing in any of these areas, you may feel incomplete or disconnected in experiencing the full capacity of your love.

What Is Love Not?

Now that you've been introduced to the various types of love, let's talk about what love is not. It is important to identify what love is not so that you can bring some of the unconscious beliefs to the consciousness and release any belief that no longer serves you. It's like when Michelangelo was sculpting the statue of David. He kept on chipping away at all the marble pieces that were not David to discover all that David was and still is today. That's what you do when you release limiting beliefs, and in relation to love, you keep on releasing what is not love until all that is left is what love truly is!

I have briefly touched on some of the ways that your beliefs about love are formed. This goes as far back as your childhood and even into your past lives. I shone a light on conditioning and the various ways in which you have been conditioned to seek out, receive, and experience love. Past generations have had little to no education about the difference between sex and love, and further confusion may have ensued by being told that you only have sex with someone that you love and then you end up marrying (because that was the "right" thing to do).

In my work with couples, I have seen people use sex as a way of receiving validation and reassurance and, at times, even as a form of emotional release. Yes, sex can be a way to connect and receive love, but sex is not what love is. There is a difference. False beliefs on love and sex can develop unhealthy dependencies and expectations in relationships and even promote promiscuity in teenage years in the search for love.

For example, one of my clients was fourteen when she had her first boyfriend, and he told her that she was not a good kisser. She felt ashamed, hurt, and rejected. How could she feel all of these things? She was only fourteen. However, that's not how young brains work. They don't like the feeling of shame and helplessness. It feels like death. So when the opportunity to lose her virginity came while she was on a family trip to Costa Rica, she did it, as she had subconsciously created the belief that if she was a good lover, then she would be loved.

This led to destructive cycles of low self worth, poor boundaries, reinforced shame, and feelings of rejection. It wasn't until she identified the limiting and false beliefs that she held that love is sex and sex is love that she was able to release them and move forward with the true definition of what love is.

I hope that you are beginning to see how subconsciously you can develop false beliefs that are unhealthy and hold you back from experiencing the truth of love. Sometimes these false beliefs give you moments of connection or, at best, the breadcrumbs of love, but they will never give you the depth of true love that you desire. These fragments will never satisfy you. You can find a full list of false beliefs about what love is in Chapter 11.

You may also wish to test these false beliefs to see if you hold them or not; you can watch a video on this muscle testing technique at thesovereignwomansway.com. This test will help you identify what beliefs are stored in your subconscious mind and bring them up to your consciousness.

CHAPTER 6

The Three Keys to Self Love

Once you decide that you want to experience more love and you become the embodiment of the teachings in this book, you will experience a deeper love with yourself, in your relationships, with the Earth, with God, the Creator, and with everything around you. If you want the kind of life that is filled with love, a life where everywhere you go, you radiate love, you are love, you see love and beauty in everything, if you want *that* kind of life, then there are three keys you need to master so that you can accept yourself as worthy and deserving of that kind of love. The three keys are self discipline, self worth, and self compassion. First let's talk about self discipline.

Self Discipline

When love moves through you it will dissolve everything in its path.
Love returns to love when it is filled up,
but love is infinite, and so is her appetite.
—Joanne Omer

There is an art to knowing yourself as someone who is masterful in self discipline. Someone who is self disciplined has the ability to set a goal or objective and to take the necessary and consistent measures to achieve it. Self discipline can be overlooked on the journey of love because it is more of a masculine energetic trait (logical, rational) rather than a feminine energetic trait (emotional), and love is usually connected to feminine energy. But love is wild and often can override boundaries and rational thought. You can get lost in love. So many women who I have met will let everything go in their life when they are "in love" and essentially abandon and sometimes betray themselves in the need to be loved. Love will consume them, occupy their thoughts, and direct their actions. True love needs self discipline to be experienced in a balanced and sustainable way and to create long-lasting intimate relationships.

Mastery in the realm of self discipline will test your resolve in prioritizing your needs above the needs of others. Often for those who are accustomed to being in service to others, whether it be children, partners, or parents, this is one of the biggest challenges. As a parent, it can be really hard to put your own needs ahead of those of your children; you may have to clear a lot of beliefs on what it means to be a "good" parent. Needless to say, self discipline will be required.

In the early days of my awakening, when I was still lost and didn't understand what was happening to me, I found that the only way I could stay focused and get through each day was to develop discipline around rituals and routines to support me.

So I began to follow a daily alignment practice. First I'd gather three tealight candles, a stick of incense, and a deck of oracle cards. I would place the three candles on an altar or in a space that was sacred to me. Each morning and each evening, I would light a candle held in my left hand in honor of my feminine energy. Then I would use that candle to light a candle in my right hand in honor of my masculine energy. I would then light the stick of incense from the left to the right candle and use it to ignite the third candle, which represented the Creator, or God.

Once all three candles were illuminated, I would take my awareness up to the Creator of all that is and ask the Creator to balance my mind, body, and spirit. You can find a recording of this meditation at thesovereignwomansway.com.

Once feeling balanced and in alignment, I would request that the Creator show me what I needed to know that day. In the evenings, I would give thanks and gratitude for the day and the blessings in my life. Finally I would pull a card from one of my preferred oracle card decks and reflect on what the message was for my day.

Performing this practice each day helped me immensely to develop the muscle of self discipline and cultivate the virtue of faith, believing that each day I would start to feel better and better.

It is important to practice discernment when it comes to self discipline, as many people will fall into the swinging pendulum effect and go between extreme discipline and then fall totally off the wagon. Often you set goals and are doggedly disciplined in achieving them, usually to the detriment of people around you and sometimes to the detriment of your health and wellbeing. It is these times that the pendulum can swing in a way that is unhealthy. However, when you put your mind to something, practice it as a matter of self discipline, and do it with love, it not only becomes discipline, but an act of devotion, and you start to cultivate the virtue of devotion.

The more disciplined you are, the more you will begin to know yourself as someone who follows through with what you say you will do, someone who honors your word not only to others but, most importantly, to yourself. This is the cornerstone of self love. The more consistently you achieve what you set out to achieve, the more you build an internal sense of worth and confidence. This leads to the next key to master—self worth.

Self Worth

Self worth refers to the inner knowing of your value and the sense of respect that you have for yourself. You must see yourself as just as worthy and deserving of happiness, joy, prosperity, love, abundance, money, and health as anybody else if you want to experience love. You need to know that you were born as a divine spark of light, no worse or better than any other soul. At a soul level, everyone is the same. It is from this place that you can understand that you are worthy and deserving of the life that you desire and of the love that you desire. By healing the wounds of love (more on that in Chapter 8) and recognizing your own self worth, you can attract and experience even more love in your life, which, in turn, allows you to really understand and embody worthiness at the level of your body, your mind, and your soul.

Self Compassion

Third, self compassion. You can be disciplined and you can believe that you're worthy, but if you don't have compassion for yourself, then you will get trapped in cycles of self criticism, judgment, guilt, and shame. Being kind to yourself and then, in turn, kind to others is critical in mastering self love.

Kindness, patience, and forgiveness are critical virtues to master in the realm of self compassion. Being kind to yourself as you go through life each day, being patient with yourself, and forgiveness will support you to practice self compassion.

Forgiveness involves forgiving yourself for past decisions that you may have made that have caused pain to either yourself or another. Having forgiveness and self compassion for yourself will make it easier for you to reciprocate forgiveness for those that have hurt you or caused you pain.

I believe that I chose my mother so that she could teach me compassion. I had little to no compassion for my mother's suffering even up until my late thirties. I had suppressed my own suffering and sadness for so long, thinking that I had to be strong and brave all the time. When I would lash out and say nasty things in reaction to my hurt, my mother would often wonder how I could be so mean. I was angry, and that anger was masking the hurt in my heart; it was a mask that I wore to protect myself from feeling the sadness that was underneath the bold exterior. I realized that I didn't have any compassion for myself, for my emotions, or for my feelings. I was so self critical that I had no space for compassion for me or anyone else. Once I saw the pattern of suppression of my sadness and finally allowed myself to feel it, I was able to feel more compassion for myself and, in turn, others, including my mum!

Through the integration of self discipline, the actions of prioritizing your needs and following through, knowing your value through self worth, and practicing kindness and forgiveness through self compassion, you can journey toward an empowered life filled with love, authenticity, and connection. By honoring your needs, recognizing your inherent worth, and embracing compassion for yourself and others, you pave the way for profound transformation and deeper experiences of love in all areas of your life.

CHAPTER 7

Letting Go

Love needs freedom to live.
Love cannot live in a cage.
Love cannot exist with constraint.
Love is all encompassing.
Love is everything.
When I am free, I LOVE.
—Joanne Omer

Letting Go of Identity

If you want to experience and awaken more love, power, freedom, and wisdom, you have to let go of everything that you believe that you already know about yourself. You have to let go of your attachments, your fears, your resentments. You have to be willing to deconstruct every conditioned belief that no longer empowers you or leads you toward love.

This work is not for the faint of heart. Love might feel or seem to be all rainbows and unicorns, but the truth is that to really know love, you must know loss and grief. Sometimes you have to experience heartbreak or disappointment and feel the pain again and again. The path to awakening to this kind of love is not linear. There is no formula with guaranteed results. You never know what your love journey is going to look like, but you know where to start. Finding love starts with letting go. When you let go, you pave the way for healing. So what exactly do you need to let go of?

Heartbreak

A book about love wouldn't be honest without talking about heartbreak. Unless you have experienced love and the loss of it, then you really don't know the depths at which you can love. Heartbreak can be one of the most challenging experiences you will deal with in your life. Experiencing the depths of love, connection, intimacy, and passion and then losing them brings with it the most unimaginable pain at a soul level.

Despair is an emotion associated with heartbreak and is a feeling of helplessness. When someone else exercises their own free will in their life and it is not what your heart wants, it can be difficult to understand. Feelings of helplessness and despair overwhelm you when you realize that there is nothing you can do to change the situation, to change that person.

That is why when people experience heartbreak they ask why. "Why did this happen? Why would someone do this? Why me?" You often will never truly know the reason people behave the way they do because humans are complex and intricate beings, each with their own unique genetic blueprint, soul purpose, and belief systems. So asking why will never give you the answers you seek but will only serve to reinforce the feedback loop of helplessness. Free will means that you can't make someone love you or fall in love with you.

Healing from heartbreak is a grieving process. You are grieving the love that was, that could have been, that is no longer. You are grieving the life you thought you were going to have with that person. In those moments, it is so important to allow yourself to feel that loss, to feel the sadness and pain. I know it feels as though it will never end, or that it will kill you, but it won't. Something is being let go of, there is loss, and you will experience it physically, emotionally, mentally, and spiritually, but you will come out on the other side. You will not stay there forever. There is no time limit that you can put on grief. You will heal in your own time, and it will be different for each individual.

Heartbreak is a great teacher. There is always a higher purpose to everything that happens in your life, and your job is to discover how heartbreak is helping your soul to grow and evolve. Once you learn the lessons, the process of healing can continue, and you can begin to move forward in love.

Virtues can be acquired and mastered from feelings of despair: Hope for a brighter future and to experience love again, faith and trust that it is all happening for a higher and divine purpose and in the right timing, deepening your sense of trust within yourself. Your soul knows what it wants to create, and it knows the higher purpose. It has the blueprint, and it knows the way. Let it lead.

KunYin® has allowed me to move the energy of sadness and grief through my body. Have you ever noticed that a good cry makes you feel so much better? That is because the energy is not stuck in the body anymore. Many people experience illnesses associated with the heart and lungs when they have not healed from heartbreak. Sadness, grief, and sorrow are held in the lungs and can create dis-ease in the body.

There is a saying that touched me profoundly: "Grief is just love with no place to go." When I identified grief as love in disguise, I was much more at peace with it. So rather than looking for someone to pour my love into that wasn't present in my life, I turned that into love for myself. This was in the form of small acts of self care and self nurturing, like reading a book or lovingly tending to my body with a long, warm bath, a massage, moisturizing my skin, an at-home facial, or something to move the energy with gentleness such as yoga, KunYin®, or a walk in nature.

The Art of Nonattachment

The art of nonattachment is a term that I stumbled across on my journey toward more love and freedom when trying to discover more of who I really was. To live in a beautiful state of being conscious, it's crucial to be connected but not attached; you're moving past a desire to have and control things. That is the essence of nonattachment. Note that nonattachment is distinct from detachment as detachment implies a sense of disconnection. When you detach, you can fall prey to the habit of closing your heart and then to the patterns of denial, judgment, blame, resentment, and other forms of suffering. I realized after my awakening experience back in the United Kingdom in 2022 that I no longer felt attached to the things that were once so important to me. I wanted to let go of those things to make space for my new priorities: Feeling free, alive, and knowing myself more deeply. To experience those new ways of being, I had to let go of the old ways. Old patterns and beliefs needed to end so that new ways could be created. It was during this time I had a revelation about how much I hated endings. I didn't like the thought of anything ending. I realized that throughout my entire life I had been lucky enough to not experience too many endings. My parents stayed together (not always the most joyful relationship) until my dad passed away at the age of sixty-two. My husband and I met when I was only nineteen, and we married six years later. At the time of writing this book, we have been together for over thirty years. I still am connected to most of my friends from childhood. I don't really fall out with many people. Someone had to die, literally, for there to be an ending in my life. For you, there may have been many endings through the experience of broken relationships time and time again. Regardless of your experience, it takes tremendous courage to unwind all the old patterns and beliefs that you have been demonstrating all your life.

For me to choose to change based on my own free will felt almost like the old parts of me had to die so that the new me could be born. It was there that the art of nonattachment came into my life. I realized how attached I was to my relationship and the opinions of others who might think poorly of a woman who leaves her husband and responsibilities to go away to live her passion and purpose and, in the process, finds herself!

I was attached to my own beliefs about being a wife. Good wives stay home and take care of their husbands; good wives don't travel alone. I was resentful of being a wife! Of course, I was attached to making sure that my husband was supportive of me and my new and surprising desires. He was shocked to say the least because this came as a very big surprise to him and could not have come at a worse time. His mother had just passed away and now his wife was going through what he described as a midlife crisis. It was one of the toughest times that I had to go through. In hindsight, I can see the higher purpose of it all, but, at the time, I felt like I was dying. Because no matter what I chose, someone would be unhappy. But I had to choose: Me or everyone else. I couldn't see how it was possible to make everyone happy at the time. All my strategies for pleasing, accommodating, and being flexible to find solutions were failing. I felt helpless, and I felt terrible that my desires could cause pain to the people that I loved and cared about. But at the same time, I was miserable. I wasn't happy, and my family could see this. So in the end, I chose me. But to choose me, I had to grow as a woman, no longer a little girl, a compliant or rebellious teenager running the show. I had to master the art of nonattachment.

Many people in a similar situation believe that they have no other option but to leave their relationship. I have witnessed clients paint their partners as villains so that they are "justified" to do what they please. They look for evidence to create a good case against their partner as to why they should leave or sabotage the relationship by having an affair. I was not going to do that; my husband was and still is a good man who deserved so much better than that. I had to be willing to not be attached to his feelings, to face the fact that he may choose that he no longer wanted to be with me. I had to face the opinions and constant questions from my mother, who had good intentions but whose conversations often landed with me as judgment because I was also judging myself! In essence, nonattachment is detaching from people, circumstances, and belief systems with transparency, authenticity, honest communication, and, most importantly, an open heart.

I was attached to my relationship as it was, I was attached to what other people thought of me, I was attached to my old and conditioned beliefs that no longer were a vibrational match for the woman that I was becoming. I was attached to the safety and connection I shared with my husband, I was attached to my home, I was attached to my dogs, my car, my properties, my money, my my my . . . I was so over it. I didn't want to own anything, and I didn't want to be owned. I wanted freedom to be me.

When it comes to love, relationships, and life in general, it is so easy to become attached to things, people, places, experiences, feelings, and emotions. To master the art of nonattachment (and I refer to it as an art because it is an art, there is no science to it), you must navigate your own fears and beliefs and heal your wounds of love, betrayal, separation, abandonment, denial, and judgment. I describe these wounds in detail in the next chapter.

I recently watched a group of Tibetan monks work on a beautiful mandala for seven or eight hours a day, over a period of seven days, carefully crafting grain by grain of sand, only for it to be destroyed and sent back to the earth within a few hours of being completed. For hours, I watched these monks painstakingly craft and create this beautiful mandala with incredible accuracy, concentration, devotion, commitment, patience, and strength, and I asked myself, "What could I learn from these monks? How is this a lesson for my life?"

I asked the Creator, "Why am I here to witness this?" And the response that I got was that this is what it is to live a life harmoniously in nonattachment. The monks were committed to creating this mandala, and they did it with such devotion, such care, detail, accuracy, and teamwork. Then, when it was completed, they let it go. They didn't want to stay attached to it.

To me, this is the perfect lesson in the art of nonattachment, and it is necessary for your evolution and the evolution of humanity. The more you hold on, the less you progress. When you're holding on, you're looking into the past, attached to it rather than focusing on the future. You're focusing on what you don't have or what you might lose rather than what you could gain if you let go.

Just like the monks, letting go or not attaching does not mean you are disconnected from people, places, experiences, and emotions. You are devoted to them while you are with them in the present moment, and you give them everything you have. But when it is complete, when the experience is over, when the relationship is over, you let it go and start again. Maybe it's with somebody new; perhaps it's just an experience that is gone and you are moving on to the new experience; perhaps it's a life that is incomplete after the loss of a loved one and you have to learn to move on without them. Whatever it is, let it go.

What would life be like if you lived it with this philosophy of being committed, dedicated, devoted, focused, and present and then, when your work is done, or when each task is done, or a moment is gone, or an interaction has ended, you let it go? Who would you be if you were not attached to being who everyone expects you to be?

Fears

Love is what we are born with. Fear is what we learn.
—Marianne Williamson

If the thought of nonattachment or not being who everyone expects you to be scares you just a little bit but also excites you at the same time, then you are onto something. Everything you desire is on the other side of your fears.

Your fears are the number-one obstacle that stops you from feeling and experiencing the depths of love and the life that you desire. By identifying them, you can bring to your awareness what is stopping you in your life. Many people fear intimacy even though that is what they crave the most.

A great tool that I have learned and adapted from my years in personal development is the process of uncovering the truth of your fears. Introspection and self reflection support you to uncover the depth of your fears. More often than not, what you think you fear is actually not the deeper fear.

In general, going deeper involves asking yourself a series of "why" questions to reveal deeper motivations, beliefs, and emotions.

Following is a general framework to go deeper into understanding yourself and your fears.

1. Start by identifying the fear you want to explore.

2. Ask yourself why it is important to you that you overcome this fear. Write down your answer.

3. What is on the other side of it? Write down your answer.

4. Ask yourself what is the worst thing that would happen if this fear was to occur. Write down your response.

5. Then ask yourself how that would make you feel. And write down your response.

6. Ask what would be the worst thing that could happen if you felt that way? Write down your response.

7. Continue asking the last two questions, digging deeper with each subsequent answer. Aim to reach seven levels of questioning to uncover underlying beliefs, values, fears, or desires.

8. If you get beyond seven levels without looping, keep going until you start to loop. It's important to keep going at least seven times.

9. Reflect on the insights you've gained from this process.

10. Muscle test these deepest beliefs to see if you have them stored in your subconscious.

11. If you were to be free of these fears, who would you be? What would you feel?

This technique can help you gain clarity on the source of your fears. By consciously choosing to uncover your limiting beliefs, you can make more informed choices aligned with your truth and desires.

The most common fears are the fear of poverty, abandonment, separation, failure, being judged, and, ultimately, losing love. Note: As you work through the five wounds of love in the following chapter, your fears may arise.

Resentment

Holding on to resentment is like drinking poison and expecting someone else to die. It only harms you. It can make you physically ill and can take away your joy, pleasure, and happiness in life. Underlying resentment is usually some kind of hurt or sadness. Without getting to the source of the hurt and moving through it with conscious awareness and movement of energy, it can, over time, become resentment.

I recently had a client who was going through a really rough time. All the time I had known him, he was confident, fiery, caring, compassionate, and passionate about his work. When he finally came to me, he was a shadow of his former self. He was broken, disengaged from life, and angry. His body was responding with aches and pains, inflammation and ulcers in his mouth and on his skin. When he spoke to me, I felt that he was filled with anger. Upon digging deeper, we discovered that he felt enormous guilt toward himself because he had been so preoccupied with building his new business, he had not yet visited his mother's grave overseas since she passed over seven years prior. He resented his business, his customers, and, causing the most harm, himself. The guilt, sadness, and grief was eating him up from the inside. However, his outward emotions were outbursts of anger toward his loving wife, customers, and staff. Digging a little deeper, we discovered that anger was a go-to emotion for him since childhood to get him into action and to create results in his life. In essence, his drive for success was driven by anger.

Anger is an emotion that destroys you from the inside. Psychosomatically, anger is held in the liver and can create inflammation in the entire body. Once we were able to distinguish that guilt and sadness were the source of his anger, my client was able to devote time to visit his mum in Iraq and, thus, let go of the guilt and allow himself to be driven by peace and connection.

Another client who struggled with resentment had a very harsh father who criticized her and mentally and physically abused her. Despite this, she was incredibly successful in her business! In fact, she was one of the top salespeople in her company. When doing a healing session with her, we discovered that her resentment toward her father drove her success. She would work hard to avoid criticism, to prove to people how valuable she was, and it pushed her to great heights. However, it was still resentment, and it was taking up space where love could reside. Once she was able to discover how the resentment had served her, she found alternative ways to be driven. Resentment takes up a lot of energy that could be best used elsewhere, and it always takes up the place of love! You can't be loving and resentful at the same time.

What or who do you resent that is taking up unnecessary space in your body, mind, and soul? Are you ready to let that go?

Addictions

When you usually think about addictive behaviors, you might think about drugs, sex, alcohol, food, or smoking. In this book, I refer to addictions as any repetitive, unconscious behaviors of avoidance or dependency. Allow me to elaborate. As I have spoken about in earlier chapters, subconscious patterns and behaviors govern a large percentage of your life, how you think, feel, and behave. In the case of addictive behaviors, I invite you to go a little further and look at what subconscious habits you have been consistently running that enable you to avoid how you are feeling. What do you do to fill a space in time? For example, I noticed that whenever my partner finished a job and was back in his car, he would call me, not for any particular reason or with anything to communicate but as a way of reaching out for connection. Often these calls would end in arguments or disagreements. After having a conversation about this, we realized that the call was to fill a void of connection with himself. Rather than taking this time to connect with himself and feel how he was feeling, he would bypass this feeling and reach out to someone else for that connection. Often the desired outcome was not being met because what was really missing was a connection with himself. This can be a type of dependent behavior—depending on others for connection to fill a deprivation of connection within yourself.

Likewise, I noticed in my own life that I was constantly and mindlessly scrolling through social media feeds, messaging apps, and emails. They all attempt to serve as a means of connection; however, they lack the substance needed to fulfill that desire. Have you ever found yourself mindlessly scrolling and then, an hour later, wondering where the time has gone? So many people become addicted to the comments, the likes, the engagement they get on social media, getting a temporary injection of dopamine (the love hormone) only to be chasing it again minutes or seconds later like a hungry little monster that can never be satisfied.

What are some of your consistent avoiding or dependent behaviors? Where do you avoid just being with yourself, in your bodily sensations and feelings? The next time you mindlessly reach for your phone, stop, breathe, and feel into your body. Notice the feelings and sensations; relax any part of you that has tension. Notice it, and let it go with your exhale. After three minutes, feel into whether you really want to reach out to that person or whether you really want to scroll, and follow what feels true for you.

Each and every time you stop unconsciously running these habits, you build your strength and self discipline. You will find that you achieve more of what is really important and, in the process, understand yourself and your body at a much more intimate level. This is critical because being sovereign requires you to be self aware at all times, consciously moving through life, choosing powerfully what you do in each moment.

## CHAPTER 8

The Five Wounds of Love

It is love that we crave.
It is love that is the healer.
It is love that is the answer.
And love is always there.
Can you receive it?
Can you hold it?
Can you keep it?
Can you see it, experience it, and know that you are it?
Love is the very fiber of your being.
—Joanne Omer

The journey to living powerfully from love and living life on your terms requires you to do some healing. You carry emotional wounds with you through your life. And there are five wounds that are necessary to heal. To live life powerfully and to be in your truth, to truly be of service in the world, to serve the greater good, you need to heal the wounds of betrayal, separation, abandonment, denial, and judgment. Let's explore each of these wounds in more depth.

Betrayal

The first wound of love that must be healed is the wound of betrayal. This wound cuts deep and very often spans lifetimes. The betrayal wound is when you have placed your faith and trust in another, and your trust has been broken or your expectations have not been met. Betrayal includes cheating, lying, hurt, disappointment, disillusionment, backstabbing, broken promises, and gossip. Any of these behaviors can lead to feelings of betrayal, and unless those wounds are healed, they will show up most prevalently in intimate relationships, in families, and amongst women. Many women have been betrayed by the patriarchal society in which they live. Women have had to compete with each other to survive in a competitive, masculine world, where they feel they have to become more like men in order to receive the same rights. In this way women betray themselves. You forget that femininity is a gift, that its power helps you collaborate and create. Many women also have what is called the sisterhood wound. This is the wound of betraying other women in order to survive or get attention, admiration, or love. This behavior is a scarcity mentality stemming from insecurity, fear, and lack. In order to experience love, you must heal these wounds.

The way to heal the wound of betrayal is through forgiveness and trust. Even as I say it, I can feel the energy of that and how that might be landing for you. How can you trust when everything inside of you says not to trust? Trust is how you grow and evolve. It is how you acquire virtues. In order to trust again, you need to have faith, be vulnerable, and have wisdom and discernment in understanding who you can and can't trust. Forgiveness for the past and learning how to trust again is a critical piece of healing the betrayal wound. As you heal the past wounds, you will begin to develop discernment on how to trust again. You can develop discernment through the following practices:

Trust your intuition: If something feels "off," it probably is. Follow your gut instincts. Feel into your body—how does it feel about the person or situation? Listen to it. Intuition is one of the most important tools you gain from a connection with your body. When you don't have a connection with your body, that gut instinct may be overridden by your mind, which may be driven by a need for love, acceptance, or connection and lead you to make poor decisions.

Look at words and actions: Congruence in walking the walk and talking the talk is a great indicator of a person's trustworthiness. Is this person congruent in what they say and what they do? Actions do speak louder than words. It's easy to say something, but not as easy at times to follow through with consistent action. Observing congruency in others' behaviors is essential for developing discernment in trust.

Set powerful boundaries, and honor them: Don't assume everyone is trustworthy. Does another person consistently cross or violate your boundaries? People who are respectful and honor your boundaries can prove themselves to be trustworthy over time. Go through the processes above, feel into your body, trust your intuition, and observe and communicate boundaries before making any big decisions or trusting too quickly.

Do you trust yourself? This is another very important question to ask. Do you betray yourself for those that you love? Some people will do anything for love, even betray their own feelings.

Separation

Typically, when you think of separation, you probably think of physical separation such as relationship breakdowns or endings that lead to separation from the people you love. You might also think about emotional separation, where you detach emotionally or energetically from another. Separation can evoke profound feelings of loss, aloneness, sadness, grief, mourning, and a yearning for reconnection.

Those who have not healed the wound of separation will do anything to avoid its symptoms. Separation has the potential to bring about anxiety, fear, attachments, addictions, or compulsions. It also highlights areas of codependency, areas where you have become dependent on another for love, validation, attention, support, and, in extreme cases, identity.

Codependency can be an unbalanced and unhealthy relationship dynamic where one person (the codependent) excessively relies on another person for their sense of self worth, decision making, emotional wellbeing, and identity. Codependent relationships are characterized by a lack of boundaries, poor communication, and an imbalance of power dynamics. The codependent person may place more importance on and prioritize the needs and feelings of the other person over their own, often to their own detriment. Codependency can lead to feelings of resentment, low self esteem, lack of trust, and an inability to maintain healthy boundaries in relationships.

The polarity of codependency can be extreme independence. Unhealthy independence in relationship dynamics can manifest when one or both partners prioritize self reliance to the detriment of emotional intimacy and connection. Extreme independence can lead to a lack of collaboration in the relationship, an inability to receive support, and, ultimately, feelings of separation.

The healthy balance of codependency and extreme independence is interdependency, which can be characterized by the provision of healthy boundaries in support, guidance, and the fulfillment of each other's needs. In interdependent relationships, each person maintains their sense of autonomy and harmoniously supports themselves and each other.

I believe that the wound of separation has deep roots and stems from a sense of separation from oneself. Therefore, you must examine this wound from this perspective. I have found that the experience of separation is magnified when someone is disconnected from themselves, when their body and mind become separate either through dissociation from emotions or detachment from the physical sensations in the body, which can be caused by painful or traumatic experiences. Those experiencing this wound often feel alone or lonely, and they will resort to addictive habits or codependent behaviors to overcome or avoid these feelings.

Separation can originate from the moment of birth while shifting from the comfort and safety of being inside the womb to the separateness of the outside world. It may stem from experiences within the womb where the mother may have rejected the pregnancy or had thoughts of abortion. These can trigger profound wounds of separation in a human being and, if it remains unidentified, can become the ripple effect flowing throughout a person's life. However, experiences of separation do not always necessitate delving as far back as birth. For instance, a tumultuous childhood marked by emotional distance or separation from parents may have left a wound that impacts your ability to experience love and connection. As you mature and experience breakdowns in intimate relationships, the wound of separation can be retriggered, creating feelings of loneliness and fear.

Regardless of how the feeling of separation manifests, it is important to approach it from a higher perspective. This is why I previously discussed energy in the foundational chapters. By viewing everything as interconnected through an energetic web, you can understand that you are linked to everything and everyone. Therefore, it is essential to embrace the fundamental belief that you are interconnected and never isolated. You are connected to all forms of love, to the Creator, and to the Universe through energy.

To truly understand this perspective, you must elevate your viewpoint and acknowledge and surrender to all instances where you have felt separate, disconnected, or distanced from love, from yourself, from your Creator, and remember that you are always connected to everything and everyone.

Take some time to relax and find a private space where you will be undisturbed. Take a few deep breaths, maybe even use some essential oils to relax your nervous system, and allow yourself to connect with these questions:

- ♡ What was your earliest memory of feeling separate from those you love?

- ♡ What happened?

- ♡ Where were you?

- ♡ Who were you separated from?

- ♡ Was there a traumatic event that occurred? This doesn't have to be dramatic. Remember that, as a child, even being left at home with another caregiver whilst mum goes out shopping can be traumatic . . . Don't discount anything that comes to you during this time of reflection.

Take a moment and journal your thoughts and any feelings or memories that arise at this time.

Abandonment

The wound of abandonment can have a significant impact on your emotional wellbeing. It can affect your relationships, both in the quality and depth of love. The experience of abandonment can be physical or emotional, and in many cases, it can manifest in feelings of being left out, dismissed, deserted, neglected, isolated, or rejected.

If you have experienced the wound of abandonment, you will do anything not to be abandoned again; so you give yourself to relationships that are unhealthy or out of balance. These relationships can drain you and leave you feeling empty and fearful because the ghost of abandonment looms in the background, threatening to enter your life again. These wounds can be formed at a very young age and can very often lead to codependent relationships whereby you seek a level of certainty or safety from someone or something outside of yourself.

Abandonment can make people avoid being single and, instead, go from relationship to relationship or stay in unhealthy relationships because even that feels better than experiencing the hurt created by the wound of abandonment.

If you have the abandonment wound, you may have been left by your parents at an early age. I have worked with clients whose parents had to leave their country of origin and leave their children behind in order to create a better life for the family. When the parents are secure, they send for their family to be reunited. This has created an abandonment wound that impacted the children in later years. I have also had clients who were adopted or fostered because their biological parents were unable or unfit to care for them. Sometimes you look back as an adult and you may not see the impact these experiences actually had on you at the time as a young and vulnerable child. It is important to acknowledge that this was your experience, and your experiences are deeply personal. Remember that many of these wounds are created during your early years or can even be carried through from your ancestors in your genetic DNA, such as parents or grandparents who were put up for adoption or taken care of by a family member other than their parents.

The fear of abandonment can cause people to close down their hearts, afraid that if they let love in, the very thing that heals fear, they will be hurt again. This only perpetuates the negative feelings that the wound of abandonment brings.

It is necessary to heal the wound of abandonment if you are to live a life filled with love, joy, and true happiness. The healing remedy for abandonment is coming back to love and knowing that you are loved, connected at all times, and safe. You can't walk around feeling abandoned and experience love at the same time. You must make room for love. How could your life serve love at a deeper level? To whom or what could your life be of service as an act of love, thus shifting the focus away from yourself and onto giving love from a place of service without needing anything in return? I used the word "needing" intentionally because this is different from wanting. You may want something in return, but needing implies a possible codependency. Be aware of the difference here. It is only one word, but, remember, the words you use create your world.

- What is your earliest memory of feeling abandoned by those you love?
- What happened?
- Where were you?
- Who did you feel abandoned by?
- Was there a traumatic event that occurred?

Take a moment and journal your thoughts and any feelings or memories that arise at this time.

Denial

When I first discovered the wound of denial, I have to admit that it took me some time to grasp. I was in denial about denial!

What keeps denial alive is living in a fantasy world, living in an illusion. Denial makes you turn away or ignore the truth of a situation or a relationship because to face it would be too painful. You create this fantasy world or illusion because of how you want things to look or how you want your relationships to be. Denial can present as either passivity or resistance. In denial, you can be either too accepting or too controlling based on an underlying belief of how you think things "should" be.

I often see this "too accepting" form of denial when I work with women in unsatisfying or unhealthy relationships who make up excuses or justifications for why they tolerate poor behavior. Denial can look like optimism—always seeing the cup as half full. Seeing the cup as half full can be a denial of the truth of what's really going on, and your optimism can be a barrier to seeing that truth. In the past, my husband would refer to me as a "happy believer" because I was happy living in my little bubble of denial where I would allow friends or coworkers to treat me poorly, where I would tolerate rudeness and disrespect, always choosing to see the best in people. This served me for a long time and is a good quality to have, but I failed to discern whether I was being optimistic or just in denial. The two are quite distinct but are often conflated.

To help differentiate between the two, consider the following questions:

- Are you considering both the positive and negative aspects of the person's behavior, or are you only focusing on the positive aspects?

- Are you open to feedback that may challenge your perception of the person's behavior?

- Are you actively seeking solutions or ways to address any negative behaviors you have observed?

- Are you acknowledging any red flags or warning signs that may indicate problematic behavior, or are you dismissing them?

- Are you too accepting of how another just is? Or do you encourage them to change to meet your expectations?

If you find yourself constantly ignoring or rationalizing concerning behavior without taking appropriate action or seeking solutions, you may be veering more toward denial than optimism. It's essential to maintain a balanced perspective, acknowledge both the positive and negative aspects of a person or situation, and take proactive steps to address any issues that arise.

Conversely, if you constantly try to control a situation or another person's behavior with little success, you may be in denial about accepting their free will and, instead, trying to impose your view of the world upon them. These controlling patterns can be driven by fear, perfectionism, or the projection of your own ideals and beliefs. Until you can accept the truth of a situation, you can't really impact it. Denial is like having a blindfold on—only when you take it off can you really see the reality and truth of a situation or behavior.

Behavioral patterns of denial and dissociation from the body can cause you to suppress what you are really feeling. This can lead to withholding communication, lying to yourself so you don't have to feel the pain or sadness about what is really happening, or angry and frustrated outbursts of emotion. At its core, denial is the avoidance of the truth. It takes courage and strength to connect to the truth of your life.

Living in denial can prevent you from healing. Unwillingness to see truth can block healing. It can bar you from experiencing the level of love that you truly desire, having the relationships that you truly desire, and living the life that you truly desire. Denial will not lead to love.

To move from a state of denial, you must be in harmony and learn to master the virtues of acceptance, commitment, compassion, faith, patience, tolerance, and understanding. Not everyone is ready to see, hear, and know the truth; it takes the acquisition and mastery of virtues as with all the laws.

A few years ago, I was dealing with a challenging situation within our family. I was very concerned about a family member and the choices she was making. One night, I was woken from my sleep, and I was shown the truth and higher perspective about this situation. It was difficult for me to accept as I was in denial about what was happening. I had been trying to control and manipulate the situation based upon what I felt was good for her! I asked the Creator about what was happening, and I was told that the Law of Truth awakened me to show me the truth so that I could heal from this situation. I asked the Creator why they couldn't just show me in my sleep, to which I got the answer, "If I had shown you in your sleep, you would have thought it was a dream and not paid it the attention that it deserved." The Creator works in amazing ways when you are open to heal!

Judgment

Judgment lives in the world of duality, good and bad, right and wrong. Everyone makes judgments. If you didn't, you might just drive your car into oncoming traffic! Your judgments can keep you safe and alive. What I am referring to here in this discussion of the wound of judgment is the righteousness of holding on to the assessments of good, bad, right, and wrong—those opinions and beliefs that create disconnection and perpetuate the wound of separation. The wound of judgment creates disconnection from communities, relationships, and yourself. Just take a look at the havoc and separation that has been created in the world through judgment and the need to be right. I have a saying: "You can be right or you can be happy ~ choose!" Judgment leads to criticism—criticism of others and criticism of self. Self criticism impacts your ability to have compassion for yourself, which, in turn, impacts your ability to have compassion for others. If you judge yourself and are overly critical, you often magnify the judgment and then project it out onto the people around you.

Projection is a self defense mechanism whereby you attribute your own thoughts, feelings, and beliefs onto someone else. Take a look at the judgments that you have about the people around you. Now look at where you judge yourself. How is that being projected onto the people around you? This can be a very confronting yet enlightening experience!

To explore a little more into the wound of judgment, reflect and answer the following questions:

- ♡ Where have I judged myself harshly, and how has that affected my emotions and actions?
- ♡ Where have I been righteous about a particular situation or circumstance with someone, and how has this impacted my relationship with them?
- ♡ Where do I lack compassion with myself, and how does this influence my actions?

As a psychosomatic therapist, I often look at how patterns of behavior show up in the body. Through my training and my experience face-reading hundreds of people, I have discovered that if you look at the eyebrow center of a person's face, you may see a line in the center of their brow, which is from a furrowed brow. This line can be created from overthinking, judging, or criticizing themselves. Perhaps they have had an overly critical life or started to criticize themselves from a very young age. This line can be a little telltale sign, and when I see it, I wonder what's really going on inside that person and what wounds they may be carrying around.

To go deep into belief systems around all five wounds of love, muscle test the beliefs for each wound in Chapter 11. After completing the muscle testing, visit thesovereignwomansway.com for the free meditations and downloads on healing the wounds of love. Then muscle test again. See what has changed in your subconscious!

As you move through the journaling prompts and test the limiting beliefs for the wounds of love, you can support yourself with essential oils.

Essential oils are known to access the subconscious part of the brain through the olfactory system. When you inhale the potent molecules of an essential oil, it travels through your nasal cavity through receptors to your limbic system, which contains memories and emotions.

For a full list of recommended essential oils that accompany each wound of love, go to thesovereignwomansway.com.

CHAPTER 9

Matters of the Soul

What Is a Soul?

This is a very important question to ponder. I have always been fascinated with matters of the soul and curious about past lives and experiences. Here is my perspective on what the soul is and why it's important to discuss and understand matters of the soul. The soul supports your journey to see the higher perspective of your existence and the role you play in the evolution of the planet and the consciousness of humanity. I believe that a soul is your unique slice of higher consciousness. You are connected to the vast and infinite sea of interconnected souls. Together they form a consciousness. Your soul is your unique essence, who you are. This unique essence travels with you throughout your lifetimes. When you choose to incarnate into a human body, you take a piece of this soul essence with you into that physical body. You can only take a small piece of this because your soul is so vast and so light that it couldn't possibly be contained in the dense thickness of your physical body.

This soul has memory and retains feelings and emotions that you carry with you throughout your lifetimes. It is said that souls journey together from lifetimes to lifetimes to support each other to grow and evolve. I believe that you choose to incarnate as a human so that you can learn and acquire virtues through the lessons that you experience in your life. As you grow and evolve, you become wiser and you ascend in your consciousness. You use the planet Earth and your experiences here to play, to grow, to evolve. You forgot this when you came into Earth and incarnated and started to take life very seriously and experienced all the emotions and feelings that it is to be a human, which is part of the beauty of being human but, at the same time, can also cause huge amounts of pain and suffering. This is critical because, as you evolve, it is important to experience contrast—to know suffering so that you can experience joy. Once you know and experience this contrast, you can heal and evolve higher above the Law of Polarity, free yourself from the effect of the swinging pendulum, and choose to operate in the vibrations of balance and harmony. As you grow and evolve, you also impact the collective of souls that you are intricately connected to, thus evolving all of humanity. Your growth and healing really does make a difference to everyone, regardless if you are consciously aware of it or not!

When you come to this planet, I believe you choose your parents. You choose them so that you can learn the necessary lessons that you came here to learn. Now, you may be asking yourself, "Why the hell did I choose those parents?" Well, that's a really good question, and I invite you to answer it for yourself:

- ♥ What have you learned by choosing the parents that you chose?
- ♥ Why do you think you chose them?

You also choose your siblings, and your siblings choose you. You chose your physical body too. You chose what you wanted to experience in this lifetime.

Reflect on why you may have chosen your siblings and your body using the following prompts:

- ♥ Why did I choose these siblings?
- ♥ Why did I choose this body?
- ♥ What characteristics of my siblings do I love?
- ♥ What aspects of my body do I love?
- ♥ What aspects of my body have I had a hard time accepting?
- ♥ What are my siblings teaching me?
- ♥ What is my body teaching me?

Soulmates

Soulmates are two souls that are connected in an intimate relationship. Soulmates are not to be confused with soul families. A soul family is another soul you connect to as family but may not be your natural family here on this Earthly plane. It can be a friend, a sibling, or even an acquaintance that comes into your life to help you to grow and evolve. Soulmates are those souls that chose to come together in a lifetime to grow and evolve together in an intimate relationship. This relationship may last a lifetime or it may be for a specific purpose, and when that purpose is completed, the relationship may also be complete. This is important to know because often you hold on to relationships for far too long and create unnecessary suffering. On the other hand, you may give up on a relationship before all the lessons are learned. In that case, you will attract another soul to help you learn and complete this lesson so you can evolve.

There are many different soulmates available for people today. You live in a period of time where the consciousness on the planet is rising more rapidly, and to support and empower that growth, more and more soulmates are finding each other. There are many different types of soulmates, so let's take a look at each one in more detail.

KARMIC SOULMATES

Karmic soulmates, like all soulmates, are soulmates that come together to teach each other lessons. These lessons may come through from past lives, where, as a soul, you have agreed to incarnate in this lifetime and learn lessons together. Often karmic relationships can be tumultuous and experience pain and suffering. There may even be a terrible experience, hurt, or heartbreak that causes you to go into a dark night of the soul; but, in the end, they will also help your soul grow and evolve. You may not see the lesson or the gift of it at the time; you may resent the person or even the Creator. But every experience you have is leading you to where you are meant to be. There is a saying amongst some of the healing communities that I am part of: "When you are facing tumultuous times, remember that your soul is evolving." In response, learn to say, "Thank you for this lesson! What could I possibly be learning from this experience? How could this person be my greatest teacher? How do I have to behave in order to experience my life with more peace, joy, love, and fulfillment?"

Sometimes there is healing that needs to happen before you can arrive in this space. You are also learning mastery in virtues, so be kind to yourself and have self compassion as you navigate these relationships. Karmic soulmates are meant to teach you what you need to know and how to love yourself more deeply, and you must complete that karma and move forward with your life.

ALIGNED SOULMATE

An aligned soulmate is one that is aligned with you at the time you meet. While you may or may not be with this person "forever," they will teach you to grow and evolve. They are a great match for you, as you teach the other the lessons that both of your souls came here to learn. When you are with your most aligned soulmate, life will have a good balance of challenge and support. It will be challenging at times, but not too grueling—just enough for you to grow! You will learn the lessons you need to learn at a particular time. Depending on your purpose and mission, you may outgrow this soulmate and become out of alignment and separate or you may choose to continue to grow together. That is up to you and your divine purpose.

DIVINELY-MATCHED SOULMATE

A divinely-matched soulmate is one that is a perfect match for you; they complement you. While you may not be exactly the same, you both share similar beliefs and values. When you meet this type of soulmate you *instinctively* know that you are meant to be together. You may experience a deep sense of knowing each other, almost like you have met before. The dynamic of the relationship will provide a good balance of challenge and support so that you both grow mentally, emotionally, and spiritually *together* throughout *your life.*

DIVINE PURPOSE SOULMATES

Divine purpose soulmates are soulmates that have chosen to incarnate during the same time on Earth with the objective to achieve the same divine purpose together in this lifetime. And they do that as intimate partners in a relationship, whatever that relationship looks like. They are on the same path, and they will support each other to fulfill their souls' purpose together even if it is not always easy. Their common purpose will pull them forward through some of the most challenging experiences. Often these relationships will impact humanity and make a positive impact in the world. You will know you're with a divine purpose soulmate when you feel calm, centered, supported, safe, and have the same values and purpose. These relationships are rare and last a lifetime.

Divine Timing

Divine timing is the window of time that you fulfill your soul's purpose. It is the reason that your soul exists, the reason that you came to Earth. Within your divine timing can be three or four things that are predetermined before you even come to this planet. In your divine timing, you will always achieve what you came here to achieve. It will happen no matter what gets in the way; the destination is written. The journey can vary, so how you get there is up to you. But it's important to know that you will achieve what you came here to achieve. As you go about your life, releasing limiting beliefs, healing, and acquiring virtues, you are moving closer to the fulfilment of your divine timing. It's all part of the game of life! When your soul has completed its purpose, it will leave; it will exit the body and know that it is done. Now, this may not always be overly apparent to the people around you. And this can be sad when there is a sudden death or somebody passes tragically, and your humanity cannot possibly understand why or how this could happen. But know and trust that that soul could have very well sacrificed itself at a young age to teach humanity a lesson. Perhaps understanding tragedies from the perspective of how they teach people compassion impacts people at a deeper level.

Lessons and Initiations

In order for you to grow and evolve, there are times in life where there will be initiations. Initiations are not necessarily lessons; lessons you can have on a daily basis. They're a little bit more mild. Initiations, on the other hand, are deeply transformative. They trigger a spiritual awakening that connects you more deeply to your purpose and higher levels of consciousness. They can come when you least expect them and mark a transition in life from one state of being to another. At times, they are marked by experiences that plunge you into a dark night of the soul, a time when you're not sure why you even chose to come here, and you may want to exit. Those that make it through a dark night of the soul will have an extraordinary opportunity to awaken and to see things from a new perspective. Dark nights of the soul can be an initiation into the next stage of your evolution. And, remember, without experiencing the dark or the depth of your sadness and your grief, you cannot know what it is like to experience the joy, the bliss, the ecstasy that it is to live a human existence. This is what it is to be human, and, ultimately, the opportunity is to transcend this state of polarity, integrate all aspects of yourself, and operate predominantly from the light!

Timelines

Now I'm going to get a little freaky, so stay with me. Have you ever thought about the construct of time? Where does it come from? Well, I'm going to make it simple for you and tell you . . . It was made up! Time is an illusion; there is no such thing as time. It only exists in language, and, in fact, every lifetime you have ever had and every possibility for your life exists . . . AT THE SAME TIME! It is your choice what path you choose.

Did you ever watch the movie *Sliding Doors*? It's a romantic drama film that explores two parallel storylines following the life of Helen, played by Gwyneth Paltrow. The film cleverly illustrates how one seemingly insignificant event—catching or missing a train—can drastically alter the course of one's life.

In one storyline, Helen catches the train and arrives home to find her boyfriend cheating on her, leading her to start a new life. In the other storyline, she misses the train and remains unaware of the infidelity, continuing on with her current life. The movie interweaves these two timelines, showing the different outcomes and choices Helen makes in each reality. It delves into themes of fate, love, and the impact of small moments on the trajectory of one's life.

Now, try and wrap your head around that! Sometimes soul connections with people you meet can feel so strong, you are sure that that person or relationship is meant for you. You can have unexplained feelings for others that can become obsessions, and you don't even know why. You can be in a foreign place and see someone and feel and think that you "know" them. They are signs that you are on the right track, close to or in your divine timing! You are always on the right path.

It may only be a fleeting glance, a conversation, or something more intimate. Not everyone you meet in life and in these times of connection is meant to stay in your life forever. They may be crossing your path to teach you something, to bring something into your awareness. If you are not present and in the moment, you may miss it.

CHAPTER 10

Integration and Mastery

As you continue to work through limiting beliefs and move through emotions, you will heal and acquire virtues. You will enter a period of integration and mastery leading you toward your divine timing. Integration is more than knowing. The ego will tell you that you are integrated, but unless you have really done the work and are living consistently in a beautiful state of sovereignty, power, freedom, and love, I believe it's just an ego trip. As I mentioned in the foundational principles, mastery is an embodiment of the sovereign woman's way. It is where you fully embrace and heal the light and dark aspects of yourself. You are no longer taken out of life by the constant triggering of your wounds. This process can take years, sometimes even decades. Even then, as you are continually learning and evolving due to the very nature of your soul, it is an ongoing process of mastery.

I was shown by the Creator that when I had healed the little girl inside me and the rebellious and defiant teenager that was running my life, my integration would begin, and the sovereign woman inside could reign in my life. You are a work in progress; therefore, it is so important to have compassion for yourself on this journey and compassion for all the souls who come to shine a light on the areas that you are ready to heal.

Throughout my life, I have come to realize that anything great that I have ever accomplished has not been achieved on my own. Each and every time, there has been a tribe supporting me, challenging me, cheering me on, calling me out on my shit, loving me, and empowering me to connect to my intuition and make my own choices.

I truly believe that for humanity to grow and evolve in consciousness, it must adopt a heterarchical view of the world rather than hierarchical. I don't want to be your guru, I don't want you to put me on a pedestal. The intention of this book is for you to discover your own sovereign guru within, and be the embodiment of her!

Imagine a world where individuals are not bound by rigid top-down control but, instead, resemble a complex web of interconnected communities, each with the potential to influence and shape the direction of the whole. This world embodies the concept of a heterarchy, where power and authority flow in diverse and unpredictable ways.

In this intriguing landscape, traditional hierarchies give way to a dynamic network where individuals and groups can collaborate and coexist in a constantly shifting tapestry of relationships. Each individual brings their unique perspective, gifts, and abilities to the whole.

Picture a world where individuals thrive not because of strict rules and regulations imposed from above but because every individual has the freedom to reign freely in their own domain and can openly and freely contribute ideas and initiatives, creating a fertile ground for creativity and problem solving. This is the essence of a heterarchical structure—a world where possibilities are endless, and the only constant is change.

When a woman is whole, integrated, and complete, she has the ability to reign sovereign in her life and, in doing so, grants the same permission to those around her, creating a beautiful network of individuals freely living and loving in collaboration with others to raise the consciousness of the entire planet.

I wish you well on your journey. It's not an easy one, but it is worth it. I hope that you are ready to walk the path of the sovereign woman. The world needs you to create a sacred union with your divine masculine counterparts and to raise conscious children so that the planet can be a place where everyone works together for humanity and evolves harmoniously. But that's another story for another time!

CHAPTER 11

Limiting Beliefs

Love Beliefs

#	Beliefs	Check response Yes	No
1	I am a victim of love	☐	☐
2	I am addicted to love	☐	☐
3	I am afraid I will love too much	☐	☐
4	I am afraid of heartbreak	☐	☐
5	I am consumed by love	☐	☐
6	I am in love with love	☐	☐
7	I am lost in love	☐	☐
8	I am selfish in love	☐	☐
9	I am too much in love	☐	☐
10	I am unlovable	☐	☐
11	I am unworthy of a man's / woman's love	☐	☐
12	I am unworthy of being loved	☐	☐
13	I am unworthy of love	☐	☐
14	I have to be in pain to feel love	☐	☐
15	I have to be sick to feel love	☐	☐
16	I know how to live without doing anything for love	☐	☐
17	I will do anything for love	☐	☐
18	If I let love in, I will be heartbroken	☐	☐
19	It is selfish to love myself	☐	☐
20	It is unsafe to love	☐	☐

Love Beliefs (continued)

#	Beliefs	Yes	No
21	Love is a battlefield	☐	☐
22	Love is a game	☐	☐
23	Love is abuse	☐	☐
24	Love is addictive	☐	☐
25	Love is betrayal	☐	☐
26	Love is chaos	☐	☐
27	Love is consuming	☐	☐
28	Love is dangerous	☐	☐
29	Love is drama	☐	☐
30	Love is effortless	☐	☐
31	Love is envy	☐	☐
32	Love is hard	☐	☐
33	Love is heartbreaking	☐	☐
34	Love is jealously	☐	☐
35	Love is lonely	☐	☐
36	Love is manipulation	☐	☐
37	Love is my drug	☐	☐
38	Love is never enough	☐	☐
39	Love is pain	☐	☐
40	Love is painful	☐	☐
41	Love is protection	☐	☐
42	Love is respect	☐	☐
43	Love is sadness	☐	☐
44	Love is safety	☐	☐
45	Love is scary	☐	☐
46	Love is sex	☐	☐
47	Love is unsafe	☐	☐
48	Sex is love	☐	☐
49	Without love, I am lost	☐	☐

Betrayal Beliefs

#	Beliefs	Check response Yes	No
1	[Insert name here] betrayed me	☐	☐
2	Betrayal is love	☐	☐
3	Betrayal keeps me safe	☐	☐
4	The Creator betrayed me	☐	☐
5	God betrayed me	☐	☐
6	I am afraid [insert name here] will betray me	☐	☐
7	I am afraid my love will betray me	☐	☐
8	I am afraid my partner will betray me	☐	☐
9	I am afraid of being betrayed by love	☐	☐
10	I am betrayed by love	☐	☐
11	I am betrayed by my family	☐	☐
12	I am betrayed	☐	☐
13	I betray myself for love	☐	☐
14	I betray myself to keep the peace	☐	☐
15	I betray myself	☐	☐
16	I deserve to be betrayed	☐	☐
17	I have betrayed [insert name here]	☐	☐
18	I have betrayed myself	☐	☐
19	I must take revenge on my betrayal	☐	☐
20	I will be betrayed by my family	☐	☐
21	I will be betrayed by those I love	☐	☐
22	I will be betrayed if I am vulnerable	☐	☐
23	I will be betrayed if I surrender to love	☐	☐
24	If I give love, I will be betrayed	☐	☐
25	If I love, I will be betrayed	☐	☐
26	If I receive love, I will be betrayed	☐	☐
27	If I trust the Creator, I will be betrayed	☐	☐
28	If I trust life, I will be disappointed	☐	☐
29	If I trust men, I will be betrayed	☐	☐

Betrayal Beliefs (continued)

#	Beliefs	Check response Yes	No
30	If I trust my family, I will be betrayed	☐	☐
31	If I trust women, I will be betrayed	☐	☐
32	If I let love in, I will be betrayed	☐	☐
33	If trust my partner, I will be betrayed	☐	☐
34	It is impossible to trust the Creator	☐	☐
35	It is impossible to trust God	☐	☐
36	It is impossible to trust men	☐	☐
37	It is impossible to trust myself	☐	☐
38	It is impossible to trust others	☐	☐
39	It is impossible to trust women	☐	☐
40	It is safe to trust men	☐	☐
41	It is safe to trust women	☐	☐
42	It is unsafe to trust men	☐	☐
43	Love is betrayal	☐	☐
44	Men betray me	☐	☐
45	My father betrayed me	☐	☐
46	My mother betrayed me	☐	☐
47	My sibling(s) will betray me	☐	☐
48	Women betray me	☐	☐

Separation Beliefs

#	Beliefs	Yes	No
1	Connection is pain	☐	☐
2	I am afraid of being connected to myself	☐	☐
3	I am afraid of being on my own	☐	☐
4	I am afraid of being separate	☐	☐
5	I am afraid of being separated from those I love	☐	☐
6	I am afraid of my emotions	☐	☐
7	I am afraid of my feelings	☐	☐
8	I am afraid of myself	☐	☐
9	I am alone	☐	☐
10	I am alone without love	☐	☐
11	I am disconnected from myself	☐	☐
12	I am separate from the Creator	☐	☐
13	I am separate from God	☐	☐
14	I am separate from love	☐	☐
15	I am separate from my body	☐	☐
16	I am separate from my emotions	☐	☐
17	I am separate from my heart	☐	☐
18	I am separate from myself	☐	☐
19	I am separate from those I love	☐	☐
20	I am unsafe when I am separate	☐	☐
21	I doubt my connection to the Creator	☐	☐
22	I doubt my connection to God	☐	☐
23	I know how to live on my own	☐	☐
24	I need connection from others to survive	☐	☐
25	If I am connected to my body, I will feel pain	☐	☐
26	If I am separated from those I love, I will die	☐	☐
27	Separation keeps me safe	☐	☐

Abandonment Beliefs

#	Beliefs	Yes	No
1	Abandonment is love	☐	☐
2	I abandon myself for love	☐	☐
3	I abandon myself for sex	☐	☐
4	I abandon myself	☐	☐
5	I abandoned my body	☐	☐
6	I am abandoned by love	☐	☐
7	I am abandoned	☐	☐
8	I am afraid I will abandon myself	☐	☐
9	I am afraid of being abandoned	☐	☐
10	I am alone in love	☐	☐
11	I deserve to be abandoned	☐	☐
12	I have been abandoned	☐	☐
13	I will be abandoned by love	☐	☐
14	I will be abandoned by those I love	☐	☐
15	I will be abandoned by those who love me	☐	☐
16	If I give love, I will be abandoned	☐	☐
17	If I let love in, I will be abandoned	☐	☐
18	If I love too much, I will be abandoned	☐	☐
19	If I receive love, I will be abandoned	☐	☐
20	Love has abandoned me	☐	☐
21	Love is abandonment	☐	☐
22	My body abandoned me	☐	☐
23	My fear of abandonment keeps me loved	☐	☐
24	My fear of abandonment keeps me safe	☐	☐

Check response

Denial Beliefs

Check response

#	Beliefs	Yes	No
1	Denial keeps me happy	☐	☐
2	Denial keeps me loved	☐	☐
3	Denial keeps me protected	☐	☐
4	Denial keeps me safe	☐	☐
5	I am afraid of reality	☐	☐
6	I am afraid of the truth	☐	☐
7	I am in denial	☐	☐
8	I am in denial of [insert what you are in denial of]	☐	☐
9	I am in denial of love	☐	☐
10	I deny love	☐	☐
11	I deny my addictions	☐	☐
12	I deny my darkness	☐	☐
13	I deny my emotions	☐	☐
14	I deny my feelings	☐	☐
15	I deny my heart's truth	☐	☐
16	I deny my hurt	☐	☐
17	I deny my fears	☐	☐
18	I deny my light	☐	☐
19	I deny myself to become stronger	☐	☐
20	I deny myself to receive love	☐	☐
21	I deny reality	☐	☐
22	I deny the truth	☐	☐
23	I must deny the truth or I will be hurt	☐	☐
24	I must deny the truth or I will hurt those I love	☐	☐
25	Illusion is better than reality	☐	☐
26	It is easier to deny reality than know the truth	☐	☐
27	Life is hard	☐	☐
28	Reality scares me	☐	☐
29	The truth hurts	☐	☐
30	The truth makes me sad	☐	☐

Judgment Beliefs

#	Beliefs	Check response Yes	No
1	I accept myself	☐	☐
2	I am afraid of being judged for being myself	☐	☐
3	I am ashamed of myself	☐	☐
4	I am bad	☐	☐
5	I am judged by my family	☐	☐
6	I am judged by my friends	☐	☐
7	I am judged by my partner	☐	☐
8	I am wrong	☐	☐
9	I hate myself	☐	☐
10	I judge [insert name here]	☐	☐
11	I judge men	☐	☐
12	I judge my partner	☐	☐
13	I judge myself	☐	☐
14	I judge myself for how I feel	☐	☐
15	I judge others	☐	☐
16	I judge women	☐	☐
17	I know how to accept myself	☐	☐
18	I know how to live without being right	☐	☐
19	I know how to live without being wrong	☐	☐
20	I know how to live without judgment	☐	☐
21	I know how to live without judging myself	☐	☐
22	I know how to live without judging others	☐	☐
23	I will be judged for being myself	☐	☐
24	I will be judged for enjoying sex	☐	☐
25	I will be judged for feeling pleasure	☐	☐
26	I will be judged if I ask for what I want	☐	☐
27	I will be judged if I express my emotions	☐	☐
28	I will be judged if I express my feelings	☐	☐
29	I will be judged if I express my love	☐	☐

Judgment Beliefs (continued)

#	Beliefs	Yes	No
30	I will be judged if I express myself	☐	☐
31	I will be judged if I love myself	☐	☐
32	If I criticise myself, I will be accepted	☐	☐
33	Judgment keeps me safe	☐	☐
34	My desires are wrong	☐	☐
35	My love is right	☐	☐
36	My love is wrong	☐	☐
37	Self criticism drives me	☐	☐
38	Self criticism keeps me safe	☐	☐
39	Self criticism keeps me successful	☐	☐
40	What I want is wrong	☐	☐

A NOTE FROM ME TO YOU

Thank you for embarking on this incredible journey with me through *The Sovereign Woman's Way*. My heartfelt hope is that every single person on this planet discovers a life they adore, contributing to a world that is more conscious, compassionate, and evolved for future generations. I firmly believe that women will lead this conscious evolution starting with their own evolution and rippling out into the world.

As you explored the wisdom within these pages, I hope you experienced moments of clarity and deep self discovery. Remember, this journey is not a one-and-done deal but a continuous process of growth and evolution. As you evolve and learn more about yourself, you can always return to this book at different stages of your journey to deepen your understanding, heal any remaining wounds, and master your inner virtues.

If you feel like you've only scratched the surface and desire to delve deeper with me to better grasp the teachings and distinctions, I offer a variety of online tools and resources to support you. I also host in-person events, courses, and retreats to further assist you on your path. To stay connected, please subscribe to my email list at thesovereignwomansway.com.

Let's continue to walk this transformative path together, empowering each other to shine brightly and embrace our true selves fully.

With love,

To connect with Joanne or to go deeper into your Sovereign Journey,

please visit **www.thesovereignwomansway.com**

Facebook: https://www.facebook.com/joanne.omer

Instagram: https://www.instagram.com/joanneomer/

LinkedIn: https://www.linkedin.com/in/joanne-omer-94917432/

ABOUT THE AUTHOR

A leader empowering people
to live abundant and fulfilling lives.

Through her own development, including training in neurolinguistics, psychosomatic therapy, and energy healing modalities, as well as personal experiences, Joanne Omer has discovered the gift of living an aligned, purpose-driven life. A trained and experienced life coach and feminine healing expert, Joanne has been working with men and women for over ten years to take their lives to the next level, teaching them how to connect to their divine nature and align their mind, body, and spirit.

In 2019, Joanne founded KunYin® Studios and launched KunYin® ~ Feminine Energy in Motion, a healing movement modality especially for women. KunYin® is designed for women to remember their truth, the truth of their body, and to heal through love.

In KunYin® sessions, coaching, retreats, and workshops, Joanne focuses on the body, mind, and spirit. By coaching her clients to address limiting beliefs and discover and work through emotions and how they affect women's thoughts, bodies, health, and wellbeing on a daily basis, she enables them to create a truly extraordinary life.

Joanne brings an aliveness and energy to her coaching that has her clients causing results in all areas of their lives—relationships, finances, love, intimacy, spirituality, and careers.

TESTIMONIALS

**From the very first page, I was captivated by
Joanne Omer's unique storytelling.**

The Sovereign Woman's Way by Joanne Omer is beautifully written
and full of profound wisdom gained through her lived experiences.
The book provides practical guidance to inspire women to live life with
true purpose and authenticity. I could not put it down; each chapter
provides insights, inspiration, and ways to reclaim your power. I highly
recommend *The Sovereign Woman's Way* to any woman seeking to
transform and live an authentic life. —LINDA HOLLAND

The perfect book for entering a new chapter in my life!

This book fell into my lap at the most perfect time! I was about to move
in with my partner for the first time, and *The Sovereign Woman's Way*
by Joanne Omer couldn't have come at a better moment. Joanne took me
on a journey that helped me see things about love and relationships that
were completely new to me. I've done a lot of healing work, but there's
something so simple yet deeply transformative about the way Joanne
shares her insights and her distinctions. It made me realize how I've been
running my life—especially around people-pleasing, setting boundaries,
and the balance between giving and receiving. Her personal stories really
hit home and brought up memories I hadn't thought about in years but that
I needed to revisit. I especially loved how Joanne reframed boundaries. I
would often feel quite guilty about setting boundaries, and she helped me
to see them as something healthy and empowering.

Additionally, Joanne explained how even the smallest, unnoticed decisions
you make can affect you in ways that lead to suffering. If you're a woman
who doesn't know how to say no, is always saying yes, and constantly feels
exhausted, *The Sovereign Woman's Way* is a must-read. Joanne shows
you how to take control of your life in a way that feels both responsible
and freeing. Thank you, Joanne, for this beautiful gift of wisdom!
—EMMA EL-FHAKRI

www.ingramcontent.com/pod-product-compliance
Lightning Source LLC
Chambersburg PA
CBHW051159120626
46547CB00012B/1118